To:

Hi:

A

I hope you enjoy this book as much as I did doing the plays. ☺

ANSWER
ME HOME

PLAYS *from* TRAMORE THEATRE

Agnes Walsh

BREAKWATER

WWW.BREAKWATERBOOKS.COM

Breakwater Books is committed to choosing papers and materials for our books that help to protect our environment. To this end, this book is printed on a recycled paper that is certified by the Forest Stewardship Council of Canada.

A CIP catalogue record for this book is available from Library and Archives Canada.

ISBN 978-1-55081-348-7

Author photograph by Gemma Hickey
Cover photograph by Agnes Walsh. Photo has also appeared in Pamela Morgan's magazine *The Poet Painter*.

Canada Council   Conseil des Arts   Canadä   Newfoundland
for the Arts   du Canada   Labrador

We acknowledge the support of the Canada Council for the Arts which last year invested $1.3 million in the arts in Newfoundland. We acknowledge the Government of Canada through the Canada Book Fund and the Government of Newfoundland and Labrador through the Department of Tourism, Culture and Recreation for our publishing activities.

PRINTED AND BOUND IN CANADA.

MIX
Paper from
responsible sources
FSC   FSC® C011825
www.fsc.org

In memory of

MIKE McGRATH
OF PATRICK'S COVE

FOREWORD
by Andy Jones

Agnes Walsh's love for the accent and turn of phrase of Newfoundland's Cape Shore has allowed her plays to faithfully preserve one of the world's most beautiful renderings of the English language. Her passion for the older kitchen storytelling and singing traditions has allowed her to present the manners, customs, morality, social history, and folklore of this area of Newfoundland settled by Irish immigrants nearly two hundred years ago.

These plays show Agnes' passion not just for her beloved "old" Newfoundland but for the issues of present-day rural dwellers, such as conservation, out-migration, rural development, and modern family life. She shares her anger and frustration that no one seems to be listening to the cries for help from rural Newfoundland and that the *have-province* benefits have all gone to the greater St. John's area.

At the same time, her work is filled with fun. Her great dramatic skills present not only the witty characters of her own invention but also hilarious local gossip, jokes, and folk tales, seamlessly blended with reports of fairies and ghosts and topped with generous dollops of traditional songs.

In most of these plays the "fourth wall" of the theatre exists only as an occasional aid to her straight ahead, "once upon a time" storytelling desires. It is as if there is a well-made play going on just behind the storytellers into which, from time to time, they selectively step to heighten their narrative. *A Man You Don't Meet Everyday* is probably the best example of this direct narrative style. Only *To The City Of Point Lance* and *Chasing Cripple* are complete "fourth wall" entities (and both of these have stand-up storytelling and singing moments). Agnes Walsh moves easily in both worlds as she is storyteller, poet, and accomplished theatre practitioner.

Ultimately, all of Agnes Walsh's plays are deep investigations of family, but *Solo The Peddler*, *A Family Of Strangers*, and *First View of The Sea* particularly enchant us with the startling puzzles and paradoxes of courtship, love, disappointment, endurance, courage, betrayal and hope.

As production entities, these plays are ascetic and spare. A change of location is indicated by a change in tablecloth; when characters go outside, they simply walk into the audience. These minimal staging requirements perfectly suit Tramore Theatre's small, intimate venue in Cuslett, Newfoundland. It is also a resourceful response to the low-budget world of this independent theatre in a culturally cohesive area with a small population base. Happily for the audience, it has made Agnes Walsh depend on content and wit.

Taken as a whole, this collection is the theatre of record for a tiny piece of western civilization. It is the Saga of a faraway Irish settlement. It is the *Thousand and One Nights* of the Cape Shore, and Agnes Walsh is their Scheherazade telling the tales to save the life of this wonderful culture.

ANDY JONES, ACTOR & WRITER
March 2011

INTRODUCTION
to Tramore Theatre

When, in 1992, I bought a house in Patrick's Cove on the Cape Shore of Placentia Bay, I did so for several reasons. For anyone familiar with the stretch of shore that runs between Point Verde and Cape St. Mary's, one reason would be enough: the breathtaking coastal landscape. My other reasons were the beauty of speech in the people of the area and, of course, my house.

I grew up in the town of Placentia and sometimes went berry picking on the Cape Shore with my mother. Often we would stop and visit my mother's friends. Although I grew up with the Irish rhythms of speech in Placentia, I marvelled at how much richer the speech was on the Shore. There was always a strong sense of connection between Placentia Bay and Ireland. After I bought my house on the Shore and spent my summers there, my understanding of just how strong that connection was became even deeper.

My first collection of poems, *In the Old Country of My Heart* (Killick Press, 1996), focuses on the landscape of the Shore. My second collection, *Going Around With Bachelors* (Brick Books, 2007), focuses primarily on the rhythms of the speech from Placentia Bay. In the 1990s, I began a series of oral history interviews with some people from the Cape Shore. I was interested in learning the settlement history of the Shore and, indeed, of the whole bay. I became close friends with an elderly gentleman in Patrick's Cove, Mike McGrath, and Mike, to my delight, was keenly interested in and knowledgeable about the oral history of the Shore. His speech and stories began finding their way into my poetry.

Then, in 1999, Paul Rowe, an actor and writer from Point Verde, Placentia Bay, asked me if I would be interested in turning my research into a play about the Cape Shore. Paul and I received funding to write what became the play, *Answer Me Home, Stories from the Cape Shore*. We performed this play several times in the old one-room schoolhouse in Great Barachois. It was extremely well received by over-flowing crowds. Calvin Manning advised me to get in touch with Arlene Morrissey in Cuslett because she was interested in the arts. Paul had commitments in Trinity, so I knocked on Arlene's door. From there, Tramore Theatre was born. We were first sponsored by the Cuslett-St. Bride's Come Home Year Committee. We remounted *Answer Me Home*, hiring Mildred Dohey, Arlene Morrissey and Camilla Newman.

Since 1999, I have been the sole writer and artistic director for Tramore, Arlene has been the administrator, and Mildred Dohey our main actor and storyteller. Our core has held fast. The Cape Shore Folk Arts Council was instrumental in helping Tramore stay alive in the early years. In 2003, we formed our own production company, Tramore Productions, and have run under that banner ever since. All the early plays presented in this collection were written by me and are based on the oral history of the Shore. My plays are frequently based on oral history but other voices come in too. I sometimes write dialogue that does not come directly from the stories I collected. *Solo the Peddler*, for instance, is based on a real person, but I took some liberties with his life story and used the facts creatively. The later plays in the book deal with more modern-day themes such as family dynamics, old age and out-migration. I am also interested in the physical and psychological health of people, and so I tend to write those aspects of life into my plays. Though my plays are based on oral history and aspects of real lives, they are fiction.

In the early days of Tramore, I introduced the work of the Irish playwright John Millington Synge into our repertoire. Synge wrote his plays based on the speech of the people from the Wicklow Mountains and the Aran Islands. I thought that speech would sound beautiful in the mouths of Tramore actors, and I was right. In fact, one evening there was a Synge scholar from the United States in the audience, and he asked me who our dialect coach was!

In 2002, I was invited to Bere Island in West Cork, Ireland, to help start a theatre troupe based on the Tramore model. I brought the Bere Island actors to their feet with Synge's *In the Shadow of the Glen* and, in turn, invited them to come over to Cuslett to perform another Synge play. In 2003, The Bere Island Theatre Troupe performed on the Cape Shore to sold-out audiences. In 2005, I went to the Aran Islands to watch the Druid Theatre Company of Galway perform all of Synge's plays. It was a very memorable and moving experience for me.

It has always been an exciting challenge to write and direct for Tramore. I have also found it rewarding to work with Arlene Morrissey. Over the years she has donned many hats: administrator and general manager, seamstress and costume designer, bookkeeper and stage-manager, front of house and public relations. Arlene kept me grounded when I had a myriad of ideas for Tramore, such as wanting to get a horse and caravan for Tramore and hit the roads of the island with our plays.

In 2005, Tramore was invited to perform in Ireland by the Festival of the Sea. We performed in Waterford, Wexford, and Kilkenny. We chose the play *A Man You Don't Meet Everyday* and had the opportunity to perform it in Tramore, County Waterford. This was very meaningful to us because our name has a direct link to that seaside town. It is said that one of the first settlers on the Cape Shore was a Thomas Foley, and he was given the nickname Tramore after the town he came from. I thought it fitting to name our troupe after an early settler whose nickname came from the southeast of Ireland.

I feel very fortunate to have been born in a time and place so rich in oral history and musical culture. I left Newfoundland as a teenager and returned in the mid-seventies. It was a good time to be home. Figgy Duff was playing, collective theatre was hopping, and Newfoundland poets were being recognized and published. The islands in the bay had been resettled, Joey was gone, but the old ways held on for a bit longer. Meeting Anita Best, Patsy Judge, Emile Benoit, Carrie Brennan, Val Ryan and Andy Jones, to name but a few, was the best education a writer could get. They were and continue to be my inspiration.

In closing, a word about the title: *Answer Me Home* was a pre-Tramore production written by myself and Paul Rowe, and was the catalyst for forming a theatre troupe on the Shore. We (Breakwater and I) chose not to include the play in this collection because it was pre-Tramore and because some of the stories from that original play have been re-set in another play, *Just Ask Rosie* (which has been included) and have been told separately as stories in storytelling sessions by Tramore.

That being said, I wanted to use the title because I love the expression. Its origin comes from people in small communities gathering to tell ghost stories late at night, before electric lights could guide a person safely (from spirits) back home. The person leaving would ask the host to keep talking until he or she was safe home. "Answer me home, go on, keep talking. Okay, I'm home now. Goodnight."

LIST OF PLAYS

TO THE CITY OF POINT LANCE

Approximately 45 minutes

To the City of Point Lance was first produced in 2001 in the Cuslett Community Arts Centre.

In the early decades of the twentieth century a young girl ships herself out to a woman-less household of fishers in a community up the shore from where she was reared. She has her heart set on working in a big place with bright lights and dazzling people. After walking all day with her escort, a young man from the house she has shipped to, she comes into Point Lance in the dark of night. Upon arising the next morning, she goes out into a community of unpainted houses with only a handful of people. Being of stout heart and a willful mind, she digs in her heels and sticks to her job. Along the way she finds friendship, love and a home in the "city" of Point Lance.

LIST OF CHARACTERS & ACTORS (2001 PRODUCTION)

MOTHER: Mildred Dohey
MARY ELIZABETH: Lisa McGrath
EVELYN: Brenda McGrath
FRANCIS: Rodney Baker
MR. CAREEN: Mildred Dohey

SCENE ONE

A kitchen in a home on the Cape Shore circa 1930s. A woman is baking bread and humming to herself. A young girl, her daughter, enters and flings her coat into a chair. She sits herself down and exhales loudly.

MARY ELIZABETH There, that's done. And if anyone says youngsters to me this evening, I'll drop them like I done that coat.

MOTHER My, my, my. You'd think you'd reared a tribe of them with the way you're talking. What will become of you when you gets married, my child, and starts to have a brood of your own?

MARY ELIZABETH That day might never come, and anyway, there's some chance of that happening around here. There's not one fit young fellow in the Cove, sure, Mammy. They're either too fat or too thin, too stunned or too saucy. Too old or too much like babies. There's not one fellow in the place I'd give the time of day to.

MOTHER Well, my child, you're settin' your sights too high, I'd say. Men is the same everywhere. You got to take the good with the bad. Your father wasn't perfect, like I'm not, and you're not. But we got along just fine.

MARY ELIZABETH Daddy was perfect, Mammy. I'll never find a man like him anywhere.

MOTHER Well, what about Point Lance? Think you could find one to suit you down there?

MARY ELIZABETH Point Lance? What are you talking about ... Point Lance? What's Point Lance got to do with me?

MOTHER Well, I got word today from old Mr. Wilfred Careen. He sent up word with one of his sons who was on his way to Placentia. Young Francis stopped in while you were over to Nora's. His father is looking for a girl. The woman of the house died last year and they can't manage without one. He asked if I had a girl to send … I suppose you, or Patsy …

MARY ELIZABETH Don't go saying nothing to Patsy. Tell me first, Mammy. What would I have to do? How far is it? Is it a big place? How much would I get paid? Would I be able to come back home to visit?

MOTHER Slow down, girl, for God's sake. You're some eager to leave your poor ole mother now, aren't you? And you with the life of Riley here.

MARY ELIZABETH Riley? Ole Riley must have had to work some hard for nothing, that's all I can say. Oh Mammy, not that I minds, Mammy. I just wants to get out on me own and see other places, that's all.

MOTHER Well, Francis said he'd stop on the way back in a few days' time and that he'd take a girl back with him if one was ready and willing.

MARY ELIZABETH That soon! Oh Mammy, I couldn't go that soon. *(She looks around at the room and everything in it.)* I mean I have to think about it all. I'd have to have time to say goodbye to everything … and everybody. What about Nora's youngsters? They'd miss me … and I'd miss them.

MOTHER Oh, that's the way it is, is it? A minute ago you wanted to drown them and now you'll be ballin' after them.

MARY ELIZABETH *(Ignores her mother and says to herself)* To Point Lance? I'd be earning my own money, living on my own, kind of. I'd be more independent. Not have Mammy breathin' down my neck. *(Looks over at her mother)* Mammy, where's Point Lance to? Is it far?

MOTHER Well now, I've never been there. Your father's brothers used to fish off there and well, all around the Cape, you know. People walk it. It's in a day's walk. But sure, it must be a good size, Mary Elizabeth. The way the men talk about it. It must be a fair-sized place and all.

MARY ELIZABETH Bigger than St. John's, Mammy?

MOTHER Well, no. I don't think it's that big. But sure, girl, it must be a good size. Everyone is fishing. Everyone seems to be doing well with the fish. It must be bigger than here.

MARY ELIZABETH *(Excitedly)* Can I go, Mammy? Will you let me go? Patsy can tend to everything. She's big now. Almost as big as me. And you've all the boys to help. Sure, Tommy is master of the house now.

MOTHER Well, Mary Elizabeth, you're big on going, it seems, and you are the oldest. I expect it's time you were out on your own. But you've got to mind yourself over there. You can't be speaking your mind whenever you wants to in someone else's house, the way you do here.

MARY ELIZABETH Oh no, Mammy. I'll be as good as gold, I promise.

Curtain closes.

SCENE TWO
Curtain remains closed. Mary Elizabeth and Francis are walking in front of the stage. Francis is leading the way and Mary Elizabeth is a good ways behind him. She looks tired.

MARY ELIZABETH *(Calls out to Francis, who is bowed into the wind)* Is it much further, Francis? My legs are gone.

FRANCIS We're only halfway yet, Mary Elizabeth. Should I pick you up and carry you then? *(Teases her)*

MARY ELIZABETH You mind yourself, Francis Careen. I'm after plucking the eyes out of chickens twice the size of you. You'll answer to more than me too, if you comes within a square mile of me.

FRANCIS Don't worry, Mary Elizabeth. My intention is to bring you safe and sound to me father's house by dark. And it won't be dark for good on three hours yet. We can stop if you like. If you're not strong enough.

MARY ELIZABETH Never you mind about me being strong enough. I was only making conversation. Lead on. I'll keep up, don't worry.

FRANCIS We can still make a conversation. *(Waits for her)* We can take a rest on that big rock over there, Mary Elizabeth, and catch our breath. *(Two tree stumps with a rock between them is where they sit.)*

MARY ELIZABETH Yes, my legs are like sticks now. I'm afraid that if I bend my knees, they'll crack off. We can have that lunch that my mother made up for us while we're at it. *(She takes a lunch out of her coat pocket and spreads her scarf down on the rock.)*

FRANCIS It's more like a picnic with a nice cloth like that on the rock. My mother always put a white tablecloth out on Sundays. We haven't used one since she died.

MARY ELIZABETH It must be some sad to lose your mother. I miss my mammy now. I think it just dawned on me that I won't see her tomorrow.

FRANCIS *(Jumps and points)* Look at that, Mary Elizabeth! Look at the gannets divin'. The capelin must be out there.

MARY ELIZABETH Look, the whales are divin' too! I love the sound they makes when they're puffin' out all their air. Aren't they beautiful lookin' creatures?

FRANCIS *(Gazes at her)* Yes, gorgeous looking!

MARY ELIZABETH Them gannets goes down some fast, don't they, Francis? It's a wonder they don't smack into one another, they gets so close together.

FRANCIS Do you know what they does? They stuffs themselves with capelin and then they flies back to the Bird Rock and feeds their young. One time a gannet landed on our boat and she brought up about a half a dozen capelin.

MARY ELIZABETH What do you mean "brought up"?

FRANCIS You know … throwin' up. *(Demonstrates)*

MARY ELIZABETH Ugh! Francis, go on with you!

FRANCIS I'm only telling you what I saw. And I saw it more than once too. They gets so laden down with fish that they can't fly and has to take a spell. Well, they lightens their load every now and then, I suppose. It's all to feed their young.

MARY ELIZABETH They're the same gannets that we sees home. Isn't that something, Francis? My father told me that they flies all the way to South America in the fall of the year and then flies back to the Bird Rock in May month. Now my home feels as far away as South America to me.

FRANCIS We have a fine home in Point Lance, Mary Elizabeth. It's nothing fancy, but it's sturdy and clean … most of the time anyhow. And me father is a good man and me brothers are hard workers and good fellows. You won't have worry there.

MARY ELIZABETH Well, I'm glad to hear all that, Francis, and now I suppose we should push on if we're to get there before tomorrow morning. Lead the way again, Francis, and I will follow.

SCENE THREE
Tablecloth is changed to represent a kitchen in Point Lance. Mary Elizabeth and Mr. Careen are sitting at kitchen table. Francis is sitting off to the side whittling wood.

MR. CAREEN Well, it is a steady go to get here before dark. Not easy if you're not used to the marsh. And ... if you're a woman. Never mind, you're here now and you're welcome too, me child. Welcome as the flowers in May.

MARY ELIZABETH Thank you, sir. It was a fairly boggy go we had of it. I thought there'd be a road.

MR. CAREEN AND FRANCIS *(In unison)* A road?

MR. CAREEN No, me child. There's no road. What do we need roads for when all our work is done by sea. Roads is a waste of time and money. Isn't that right, Francis?

(Francis studies Mary Elizabeth.) FRANCIS! *(Roars)*

FRANCIS *(Jumps)* What? Yes, Father, by sea. No, there's no need for roads, Father. Unless you have to drive cattle or whatever, like they does on the Shore.

MR. CAREEN What? Cattle drive ... well, yes, but that's different. Ye can't take cattle by sea. That's different altogether, sure, Francis, for Christ's sake. Everybody sells their cattle to buyers, and the buyers hires men to drive the cattle over the road. You needs a road for that kind of thing. I remembers when a buyer ... James Metcalfe from Manuels, used to come into St. Bride's, and after three or four days of buying up cattle, he'd put them into one herd which would be driven by three or four men. James Doyle, Nicky Murphy and James Conway drives still. They works some hard too, because see, the cattle bolts from the main road and gathering them back is a time-consuming job. Now Metcalfe's cattle were penned overnight at Mr. Ned O'Keefe's place in Big Barasway to rest them up for the remaining drive to Placentia. Then at Placentia they'd swim across the gut and then be loaded into boxcars at the railway in Jerseyside. One time a French butcher came to buy cattle. On his arrival he started to show a $2000 cheque around, saying he couldn't get it changed, and asking people to give him cattle for a promise to return and pay them later. Now, someone at Branch come to realize that they were being swindled, so several men went after the crook, Francis, and caught up with him on the Burin Peninsula. He was on his way to St. Pierre with the cattle.

MARY ELIZABETH Yes, sir, every year there's a cattle drive through our cove. The herd is large. I loves the sound of them and the confusion. Father used to say it is like a traffic jam, whatever that is, in some big place like the Boston States or New York.

MR. CAREEN That could be, my child … now, Francis, you get that girl a cup of tea, this being her first night here and all. Your room is up at the back, where there's peace from all them snoring galloots. I'll bring up your suitcase. Francis, stop your gawking and serve her the tea.

Francis puts the tea on the table and heads to the door. The lights fade and Mary Elizabeth takes the tea and heads for the stove.

SCENE FOUR

Lights up. Next morning. Mary Elizabeth enters rubbing her eyes. She mimes closing a door behind her. She sighs, sits down at the kitchen table and is silent for a moment.

MARY ELIZABETH *(To herself)* My God, eleven. I counted eleven houses. Eleven houses with not a lick of paint on them and that is Point Lance! Oh my God, where have I landed to? Sure, the Cove is bigger than this place! At least in the Cove I had Mammy and Patsy and me brothers and Nora's youngsters around me. Here I got no one ... and nothing. There's nothing. Nothing, only that ole long stretch of lonely looking beach. All that sand, and well, it is lovely, all that golden sand but ... oh my, it looks some lonely stretching out there and no one walking on it. It looks like it goes on to the end of the world. And them shacks up on the side of the hill, they're like crows perched, waiting to pitch on you. Oh my God, I'll never stand it. I wants to go home. Oh, Mammy. *(She cries softly.)*

Mary Elizabeth hears footsteps on the stairs. She pulls herself together, gets up and tends the table. Mr. Careen comes into the room.

MR. CAREEN Well, there you are, up already. I see I don't have to worry about you doing your work, my child. *(He looks up at the ceiling where loud thumping and grunts are heard. His sons are getting up.)* Have you tea on, Mary Elizabeth?

MARY ELIZABETH Yes, sir, and there's fish cooked and the bread all ready to be cut up, sir!

MR. CAREEN Good girl! We'll be at the tilts all week. Come up with something for supper every evening if the weather is good. Is our lunch packed now for the day?

MARY ELIZABETH It's already in the pantry, sir. You needn't worry about me, sir. I'm used to hard work and taking care of men fishing. All my brothers are fishing.

MR. CAREEN Yes, and I knew your father, my child. A hard-working man. And your brothers the same. I know who you came from.

MARY ELIZABETH *(Hangs her head)* Yes, sir. It's smaller than I thought here, sir. I thought I was going to a grander place, a bigger place.

MR. CAREEN Grander? Bigger? Well, my girl, I don't know about that. *(Boots heard on the stairs)* But I knows you better get that grub on the table before you have that lot to contend with!

Lights down.

SCENE FIVE
Lights up. Mary Elizabeth is in the kitchen singing to herself. She is putting bread in rise. She hears a knock on the door.

MARY ELIZABETH Come in! *(A young woman sticks her head in around the door and looks around the room shyly. She stands at the door.)* Come in, please!

EVELYN Hello! My name is Evelyn Whelan. I work up the road. I thought I'd drop in and introduce myself.

MARY ELIZABETH Come in, Evelyn. Wait till I wipes my hands off and I'll shake yours.

EVELYN Oh, there's no need to be so formal in these parts, my dear. You won't find people shaking hands around here.

MARY ELIZABETH Well, have a seat! I suppose I was

just so glad to meet a girl my own age, I got excited. Where do you work to? Where are you from? Have you been here long, Evelyn?

EVELYN *(Laughs)* Slow down, girl. You're making me dizzy. I works up the road a bit, I told you, for old man Bart and his crew. And I've been there six months and a bit ... a bit too long. What was the other question?

MARY ELIZABETH Oh I don't know, it'll come to me later, I'm sure. Can I get you a cup of tea? What do you mean by a bit too long? Don't you like the house you're in? *(She gets the tea ready and gives it to Evelyn.)*

EVELYN Thanks! Have you got any bickies? *(Mary Elizabeth puts some biscuits on a plate and lays them in front of her.)* Oh the house itself is just grand. Just some of the ones in it I'm not fond of. More of them I am. I'm a slave there, girl. The old man is as strict as a bishop. And some of the fellows thinks I'm a machine. "Here, mend this," says one. "Here, wipe that up," says another. "That's not fit to eat," says yet another. And that's all at the one time, mind you. I'm getting out just as soon as I sees my way clear, I tell you.

MARY ELIZABETH Oh don't go leaving any time soon, Evelyn. I think myself and you could keep each other grand company, especially with the men away all week. We'd have plenty of time to have long chats.

EVELYN *(Laughs)* Plenty of time! My God, girl, this must be your first place, is it? You won't have time enough to run to the outhouse when you needs to, let alone have a tea party with me. What with all the baking and washing and ironing and scrubbing and cooking and sewing. Although I must say, the crew you're in with is a nice bunch, the best in the place. And I'm in with the worst in the place, or near on. *(Feels sorry for herself)*

MARY ELIZABETH *(Goes toward Evelyn and pats her hand)* Now, Evelyn, we'll get some time, just you wait and see. We'll get a couple of hours off on Sunday, and after mass we'll take walks up over the hills or down by that nice river that flows into here. We'll be a comfort to each other. Even though I have a good place here, I misses my home something fierce. *(She jumps up.)* Now, I have to get the clothes hung up in the lovely sun and wind. Come out with me to the clothesline.

EVELYN Come on then and I'll help you hang them if you tells me how you gets your bread to rise so nice.

Both girls exit arm in arm. Curtains close.

SCENE SIX
Mary Elizabeth is in the kitchen. Francis is sitting on a chair whittling a piece of wood. Mary Elizabeth wipes off table, etc.

FRANCIS What are you going to be bringing up to the tilts tomorrow, Mary Elizabeth? Do you have something fancy that you made and are hiding from us? I smelt something when I come in like a spicy cake.

MARY ELIZABETH And where would we be getting any spices around here, Francis? Did a boat come ashore from Africa or something and have a cargo of spices aboard her?

FRANCIS Oh yes, girl. It come ashore and there was a hundred black men come off her and they laid down twenty great trunks all chock full of spices running out of them.

MARY ELIZABETH Oh, I see! And I suppose them trunks was loaded down with gold too, and you got it all stored up under the house.

FRANCIS There is no under *(Motions under the chair with his hand)* in this house, Mary Elizabeth, in case you haven't noticed.

MARY ELIZABETH Well, I've more to do besides crawling around on me stomach checking to see if there's a bottom to the place, or if it's stacked up with gold.

FRANCIS You're a good hand at cooking and cleaning, Mary Elizabeth. And you seem to enjoy it here too. But you won't give me the straight time of day at all. I can't tell whether you likes me or can't stand the sight of me. You're the hardest person to figure out that I ever come across.

MARY ELIZABETH So, you come across a big lot of girls in your time, have you, Francis Careen? You're what they calls an expert, are you?

FRANCIS You see what I means? That's what I means. You either won't give a straight answer or you answers everything I asks with a question, so I'm not going asking you another thing. I'll tell you, just in case you don't know, that tomorrow is St. Peter and Paul's Day. When Mother was alive she used to come up to the tilts with a big basket of stuff. Besides the stews she'd have cakes and tarts and puddings. All the women came up, but I expect you knows by now from Evelyn or Annabelle.

MARY ELIZABETH Yes, Francis, I've got it all done. But I can't be telling you what the food for the feast day is now, can I? Then it wouldn't be a surprise or special at all. And the weather will be fine, won't it? Just look at that sunset. "Red sky at night, sailor's delight ..."

FRANCIS Oh, it'll be a perfect day tomorrow, Mary Elizabeth. Perfect in more ways than one.

SCENE SEVEN

Mary Elizabeth and Evelyn are walking arm-in-arm with baskets on their arms.

EVELYN Even though we have to work it feels like a holiday, doesn't it, Mary Elizabeth?

MARY ELIZABETH Yes, indeed it does, girl, especially wearing our good dresses like we are! And Francis told me that whatever fish they catches they donates to the church. I do feel a bit odd though, Evelyn, with my hair done up and you with a bonnet on to go out to work.

EVELYN Oh sure, but the work will feel more like fun today. Everyone will be in good spirits. Even ole man Bart might take the scowl off his face or at least let me enjoy the company and the holy day. So what's all this Francis talk you're gettin' on with lately? Are the two of you courtin' then?

MARY ELIZABETH Courtin'? Some chance of that. I am not interested in Francis James Careen! Not that he isn't mannerly or kind. He even has a good head on his shoulders.

EVELYN Yes, and that head isn't a bad shape at all now, is it? Or the face that's plastered on to the front of it! Is there anything else about him that appeals to you, Mary Elizabeth?

MARY ELIZABETH Evelyn, stop talking like that, and with him up the road there, look! I am not intending to spend the rest of my days here, although I like it more than when I first came.

They come upon Francis on the road. He takes his cap off to them. Evelyn elbows Mary Elizabeth, who promptly elbows her back.

FRANCIS Good afternoon to ye, girls! And aren't ye both looking like two wildflowers in a summer field. You wouldn't be having any rhubarb tarts in either one of them baskets now, would you? Perhaps I can take a load off your arm there, Miss Whelan?

EVELYN It's not your arm nor the arm of any young goat here in Point Lance that I'd be interested in giving this precious picnic to, I can tell you that much, Francis Careen or Francis James Careen, I should say. *(Mary Elizabeth elbows her.)*

FRANCIS Oh! Well, you seem to know a good bit about someone you wouldn't give the time of day to.

EVELYN Well, I do believe that this is the first time in the near year that I've been here, Francis, that you have even looked sideways in my direction, which leads me to believe that it isn't to my aid that you're coming.

FRANCIS It's a good thing then, isn't it, that I never stopped you on the path before, seeing as how you're not so keen on the Point Lance lads. You better not go drinking the water in Point Lance then, Evelyn, for you knows what they says about that, now, don't you?

EVELYN I believe I do, Francis. Don't they say that if you puts that water to your lips, it'll turn you into a silver-throated liar right on the spot!

Mary Elizabeth is taking a drink of the water to her lips.

FRANCIS *(Looks at Mary Elizabeth)* No, Miss Whelan, that's where you're wrong. It is said that once you drinks the water in Point Lance, you'll never leave! *(Smiles at Mary Elizabeth)*

SCENE EIGHT
Mr. Careen enters.

MR. CAREEN So, there ye are. What are ye doing
dallying about down here by the Spout? I expect the other
lads will be looking for that food soon, young ladies.

EVELYN Good day, Mr. Careen. We were only having
a bit of a chat. Talking about how fine a day it is for
St. Peter and Paul's Day.

All hands sit down.

FRANCIS We were having a cod with one another,
Father. Telling stories, like the one about the water in
Point Lance. Tell us a story, Father. One of the ones you
tells us in the winter months, to pass the long nights.

MR. CAREEN A story? Ye wants a story? Well, I was
thinking of something as I was coming down the path.
Thinking of something that happened. Something I can't
get out of me mind. And, Francis, you're after hearing this
a hundred times, but if you hear it a hundred and one then
perhaps you'll only learn from it because it's a true story,
and I can testify to that. Do you want to hear it or what?

MARY ELIZABETH Yes, Mr. Careen, tell us. We're all
ears. I loves a story.

EVELYN Yes, Mr. Careen, tell us!

FRANCIS Go on, Father.

MR. CAREEN Well, it's all about a great injustice that
was done to me. It is concerning a wreck at Lear's Cove.
It is photographed in my memory and perhaps in the
memory of everyone else connected with the story. It
concerns the schooner owned by the Bests of Tacks Beach,
the *Maude Best*, which was wrecked at Lear's Cove on

December 31st of that year. The news of the wreck came to Point Lance on New Year's Day. Edward F. Careen, John T. Careen, Stephen Careen, James Nash, Fred Careen, George McGrath and myself left Point Lance and arrived at Lear's Cove at 3 p.m. that evening. A crowd from St. Bride's were already there. Among them was Constable Behan, who was stationed at St. Bride's to maintain law and order as well as to dish out the dole.

MR. CAREEN The ship was a total wreck. The rails and gunnels were chopped away. The schooner had a load of cod liver oil, and in the hold was a cargo of dried cod, which was as good as any fish I have ever seen. We helped unload the cod oil and fish, which was stored in a building, presumably belonging to Arthur Young's house. Myself and a companion went aboard the ship that evening and entered the forecastle. We got a meal of salt meat that was in the larder. I recall there was a deck of cards on the table and the forecastle was spotlessly clean. We boarded the schooner again the next morning. I took three fathoms of an inch-and-a-half rope for a dray backband. This represented all we carried home to Point Lance the next day, a journey of ten miles.

MR. CAREEN One week later, John Joe Conway and Constable Behan arrived at Point Lance. Behan took statements from us concerning the wreck. Two weeks passed and Constable Behan then issued us a summons to appear in court on February 5th. Now, the first day of February was dole day. We had to travel to Branch to get that mere dole. My trip was fruitless as Constable Behan refused to give me my order without stating a reason. I travelled back to my family empty-handed. On February the 4th we travelled to St. Bride's in order to be on time for court on the morning of the 5th. At the court hearing, we were accused of wrecking and plundering the ship. We had never been to court in our lives and knew nothing about court procedures. Magistrate Mike Sinnott and

Constable Behan were well aware of our ignorance in
these matters. Someone advised us to plead guilty and this
we did, thinking it was the right thing to do. Magistrate
Sinnott passed the sentence on each of us at thirty days
in jail. We were placed under the custody of Thomas
Conway who lived in St. Bride's, on Branch Road.
We were to remain there for the night and be conveyed
to jail at Placentia in the morning.

MR. CAREEN Now, I had to leave a wife and two small
children behind, a third would be born in a few weeks.
I had a barn with cattle, sheep, and a horse to be tended.
Wood had to be chopped and water to be brought. After
the court, I asked Magistrate Sinnott's permission to see
my sister-in-law because I wanted her to stay with my
wife while I was away. I explained my wife's condition
and Sinnott's answer to me was, "What difference is it to
me? I didn't do it."

MR. CAREEN Next day Constable Behan started to
look for horses that would take us to Placentia. First he
went to the people that were on the dole, thinking he
could force them to go, but he was sadly mistaken.
Richard Dohey and James Foley were regular drivers and
not on the dole. Constable Behan asked them to drive,
but was lucky to get away from their doors without a
trimming. Eventually, three men from St. Bride's, non-
dolers also, agreed to tackle their horses and haul us to
Placentia. Perhaps these men were in need of a dollar and
how it was earned was not important. We arrived at the
Placentia courthouse at 3 p.m. in the evening. Nicky
Murphy of St. Bride's was also with us. We were con-
signed two to a cell. Each cell had two beds. Each bed had
one grey blanket and some kind of old mattress. Sergeant
Carroll was in charge of the jail. He was a very religious
man who went to mass every morning. He would serve us
breakfast on his return from mass. Meals were scanty and
we soon felt the pangs of hunger. After three days locked

in the cells, Sergeant Carroll would permit us to exercise in the day room. Fred Careen got us permission to visit the Spout and bring water to Sergeant Carroll's house.

MR. CAREEN One day Fred met Gus Mooney Senior and told him how hungry we were. Gus, God bless him, smuggled us up many a loaf of bread. Unfortunately, he was spotted and given a warning to stop. There was some dried fish in the day room and we ate much of it raw. Sergeant Carroll noticed the salt fish disappearing and had it removed from the room. There was a tub of old fat and fried rashers, and when we got really hungry we ate them. There was also a sack of hen feed, which we mixed with water, and when we really got hungry, we ate that. Finally, on March 5th, Sergeant Carroll told us we would be free men at 11:30 a.m. that day. We asked permission to leave at 9:30 a.m., but this was not granted. At 11:30 a.m., Sergeant Carroll bade us goodbye with a stern admonishment to be good citizens and commit no more vandalism or our next term would be more severe. We had just reached the Blockhouse Hill in Placentia when hunger pains were felt. Fred Careen and Nicky Murphy and myself went into Paddy King's where we were given some bread and molasses, which we ate as we walked along. At Point Verde we all ate dinner at Tom Greene's. In all of the coves of the Cape Shore we received bread and molasses to eat on the forty-five mile journey. We arrived at St. Bride's after dark that evening. Nicky Murphy and myself were lousy even though we had obtained a clean shift of clothing from home while we were in jail. So that'll give you an idea of how poor people were treated. But that's all water under the bridge now. I was thinking of it as I was coming along. I thinks of it now and then, to tell you the truth.

EVELYN My God, Mr. Careen. Sure, ye were treated worst than animals! I'm going to tell you a story now. I'll tell ye a scary one to take your minds off poor Mr. Careen's story. Now this one was toldt to me, so I'm only telling you what I was toldt. It was toldt to me by a woman I knows, and I'm not going mentioning any names, or any places. But the story goes that there was a river in this community, and when the river was high, you had to swim across it to get to the beach. Now one time there was a bunch of youngsters out swimming across the river, and they saw a woman sitting on the barachois, you know, that part where the river meets the sea? Well, she was sitting on the water just as calm as she could be, and she called out to them to come down to where she was. They didn't know what to make of her sitting there like that. She kept beckoning to them. She had a charming manner and a beautiful speaking voice; it was half poetry and half song.

EVELYN Her hair was all golden and her shoulders were square and delicate. With one long arm she motioned to them, but they wouldn't go. They talked it over and they decided to keep on swimming across the river to the beach. But one boy broke away from the rest, and he started towards her. They all threw up a cry of alarm after him, but he kept on moving away from them and out to sea towards her. As he got closer to her at the barachois, she moved off. He went further and so did she. He floated in the current till he came to the barachois. There the current drew him under and the woman disappeared. He never came up and was never seen again. His body was forever lost. The children ran home and toldt the adults that the current drew the boy under. They never mentioned the woman. I suppose they were too afraid to, or maybe they weren't sure of what they saw.

MR. CAREEN Well, well, my dear. That was a good story. Yes, there's lots of ghost stories on the Cape Shore. Now we should be gettin' up to the tilts. *(He starts to stand up to go.)*

MARY ELIZABETH I have a story I'd like to tell too, if ye don't mind delaying for a bit longer.

MR. CAREEN Well, I didn't think ye young people had a story in ye. Tell away, me girl!

MARY ELIZABETH Once upon a time, not in my time and not in your time, there lived a princess. Now this princess lived in a house, and it wasn't a great house and it wasn't a mean house either. She lived with her mother and her sister and her two brothers. Her father, God rest him, passed away when the princess was only a young child. But this princess, who everyone called Bridie, whose real name was Bridget, remembered her father as clear as she remembered each and every sunny day. Often her mother talked about her father and how he worked hard at the fish. And how in the evenings he worked hard again at the hay and whatever else needed to be done about the land. He was a good man and a kind man, and he never let a cross word pass his lips. That's what Bridie remembered.

MARY ELIZABETH Well, it wasn't long before the princess grew to be a tall and strong young girl. She helped her mother out around the house and in the garden, tending to the animals and the hay and whatever else needed to be done about the place. She was a good girl and a responsible girl. If the princess had a fault at all it was that she was an excitable type of girl. She was prone to get enthusiastic. Oh, not hysterical, you know, not prone to a kind of flaring up type of behaviour, but more that if a bee got in her bonnet, then she just had to wrestle with it till she got it out. But she was never brash or saucy. Well, one day she had a vision and we'll leave it at that.

MARY ELIZABETH Bom by, the princess got used to tending on herself and the whole household. She took it all in stride and did all the work that came her way. But after a while she started to daydream. Her mother would come downstairs and find her hove off by the side of the fireplace, and there'd be a glazed look about the princess's face. Her mother would say, "Daughter," she'd say, "whatever are you thinking about?" "Oh, nothing," the princess would reply. This went on for some time, and the mother got worried and a little mad too because, you see, the princess had started to slack off in her duties, and well, nobody in the house appreciated that, for it took a lot to run a house, especially with her father gone. So the mother let this go on for some time, and then she had to speak her mind. "Daughter," she said, "you seem to be in an awfully strange mood these days." "Oh no," said the princess, "I'm not in a strange mood, Mother." "Well," says the mother, "Seems to me that you are, and it is so strange a mood, you don't even know you're in it." Well, the princess just sighed and went back to staring into the fire. Now, this went on for weeks, ladies and gentlemen. It went on and on. One day, the mother, she decided to get some help on the matter so she called in on the local wizard.

MARY ELIZABETH The local wizard was hove off too, only he wasn't staring off into the fire. No, he was looking into his new crystal ball when the mother walked in after knocking. "Ah," said the wizard, "I was expecting you." "Well, I come about me daughter," said the mother. "She seems terrible preoccupied these days. Can you tell me what's on her mind?" "Seems to me," said the wizard, "that you already know what's on her mind, if you don't mind me saying so." Well, the mother got to thinking about this, and so she said good-day to the wizard and dropped a coin into his cup by the door on her way out. You see, it wouldn't be very good to not tip a wizard, even if he didn't help you very much, because wizards are unpredictable and moody and could throw a spell after you when you left if they got in a bad mood. Anyway, the mother went off back towards home, and on her way she stopped to have a look out over the ocean from where her husband used to fish. She stared and she stared, and she thought and she thought, and before long a young fellow came by and he said to her, "Excuse me, missus, but could you tell me whereabouts here I might be able to find a girl for hire?" "A girl for hire?" asked the mother. "Yes," said he, "a girl to be shipped for a year and a day. And if at the end of that year and a day she likes it, she can stay forever and she'll be treated well too."

MARY ELIZABETH Well, the mother went home and she told her daughter there was a job for her in a nearby kingdom, and well, the princess got excited. But she got nervous too. She wanted to go and she didn't want to go. She thought about it and then she didn't think about it. Finally the day come when she made up her mind to try it out and go. So she did and when she got there she liked it there and she didn't like it there. Oh, the family was nice enough and the money was good enough. But she was sometimes lonely for her mother and her sister and her brothers and the place she left behind.

EVELYN Oh stop, Mary Elizabeth, it's too sad.

MR. CAREEN Well, that's quite the tale there, my girl. I never heard the likes of that before. I think it is time we were heading up to the tilts now, to say the rosary and have a bite to eat.

FRANCIS Hold on there one minute, Father. I have a story too that I'd like to tell.

MR. CAREEN Well, well, there must be something more in that water today than what there usually is. All hands has stories to tell, it seems. Go ahead then, Francis.

FRANCIS Well, my story happened a long while ago. It wasn't in my time and indeed it wasn't in your time either. But in times long ago there lived a wandering young fellow. He left home at an early age with the dream of seeing foreign lands, lands with milk and honey flowing and palm trees blowing in the warm breeze and with spices pouring out of big, fat trunks made of gold. Oh yes, he was determined to see all that, but the thing is, he couldn't wander very far at all. No, in fact, he could only wander up and down the coastline of the Cape Shore because, you see, he was a fisherman like his father and his father before him. He only travelled in his mind and in his mind, there were wondrous places. Places where big elephants roamed. But these big elephants were really the clouds that blew across the sky in one of the August breezes. Oh he saw chests full of gold, yes, indeed, only they were lobster pots in the spring of the year. But he kept up his travels because they made him happy and he thought he might run into a few people along the way.

FRANCIS So anyway that was all very good. He travelled and he travelled, he thought and he thought, and he dreamed and he dreamed till one day his father come up to him and said, "Laddo," he said, "you're gonna have to go land a girl and get her shipped. Tis too hard to manage on our own." So off he went. And as he went on his way he met all kinds of girls, oh yes he did. He met over three hundred and sixty-five girls, one for every day of the year. And not one even suited his fancy. Oh, some were as beautiful as rays of sunshine, and more sharp as blades of grass, and more wonderful cooks and able to make stoves shine and bread rise. But none was able to do what was in his mind. One day on his travels he was helping an old fellow mend his nets when a young girl come by and she started talking to him. Oh, she wasn't bold, but she set to asking him all kinds of questions about his travels, and she started telling him all about the places she'd been to in her dreams. Well, he took a shine to her in a big way and he tried and he tried to win her heart, but the girl was stubborn and self-willed and independent. And all that only made him like her more. But he feared she'd never go for him and so he travelled on back home to from where he came. And that's the end of my story.

EVELYN Well, well, well, another sad story, but by the sounds of it I'd say two sad stories could make one happy story someday. *(She elbows Mary Elizabeth.)* Now, Mr. Willie, I got a funny feeling you might be looking for another girl to be shipped as I'd say there's going to be another house built in Point Lance be this time next year. Come on, sir, let's me and you walk up to the tilts and have a bite to eat. They'll come on bom by.

Evelyn and Mr. Careen walk off arm-in-arm. Francis and Mary Elizabeth sit shyly for a while.

MARY ELIZABETH That was an awfully sad story, Francis. It took a lot of imagination to think up all that. Is that what's really important to you, someone to talk to?

FRANCIS Sure, what else is there, Mary Elizabeth? If a man and a woman can't talk and share their dreams, there's no point in being together. At least that's the way I sees it.

MARY ELIZABETH Yes, Francis. Many a long winter's night was passed with sharing an idea.

FRANCIS Maybe you and me could talk over the summer … and into the winter, Mary Elizabeth. Maybe we could get to know one another and then Point Lance mightn't seem like such a small place to you at all.

MARY ELIZABETH No, Francis, it might not after all. Now let's go and try some of that spicy African cake.

Mary Elizabeth and Francis smile at each other, get up and he offers her his arm, which she takes. They walk off together.

A MAN YOU DON'T MEET EVERYDAY

Approximately 50 minutes

A Man You Don't Meet Everyday was first produced in 2002 at the Cuslett Community Arts Centre and again in 2005 in Waterford and Wexford, Ireland.

Bride and Patsy (Patrick) Judge were always well known on their native Cape Shore for their singing and their hospitality. They were also legendary in the folk music scene of the 1960s, 70s and 80s, having songs from their repertoire performed by the likes of Figgy Duff. They were interviewed and recorded by such folklorists as Kenny Goldstein and Aidan O'Hara. This play is the story of their everyday lives as well as their lives as singers. It also portrays the times they lived in and the hardships, fun and music that was their world. Old style traditional ballads are performed throughout the play.

LIST OF CHARACTERS & ACTORS (2002 PRODUCTION)

OLD BRIDE: Mildred Dohey
YOUNG BRIDE: Judith Morrissey
PATSY: Christopher Young
ANTHONY: Mildred Dohey
WOMAN #1: Mildred Dohey
WOMAN #2: Judith Morrissey

A male voice sings off stage "The Forest Was Covered With Bushes."

OLD BRIDE *(Sings part of a song)* "... here's adieu to false lovers forever." All them ole songs they used to sing back then. That's a song Patsy used to sing. Let me tell you how I ended up with my Patsy. I was born in Patrick's Cove. Me mother was Selina McGrath from the Cove and me father was Andrew Miller from Placentia. We moved to Placentia, I think, in 1909. I was only a baby then. Father worked in the mines in Sydney, Nova Scotia, and for a while, we lived there with him. But Mother wouldn't stay. She didn't like it, I suppose, so we moved back to Placentia, right there next to the courthouse. Jackie Careen's house is there now. That's the land she sold to Jackie Careen. So we moved back to Placentia, but Father wouldn't come back, and well, Mother wouldn't stay in Sydney. Then he moved further on to the Eastern Seaboard, they calls it, in the United States. So Mother was left on the beach in Placentia with nine children. Some of them were older and could go out to work. Now Father didn't keep in contact with the family much. I suppose you could say that he more or less abandoned them there on the beach in Placentia. People along the Shore gave me mother groceries and things to help her out. But I think she couldn't take it anymore, so she got sick and ended up in the Waterford Hospital. And that's where she died in 1952.

OLD BRIDE It was back in 1919 when I was eleven years old that I moved back to the Cape Shore. I say moved back because, like I told you, I was born there, but this time I went to Gooseberry. Me mother's sister Ellen lived there. She was married to James Joe Doyle and they took me and raised me then. So I grew up in Gooseberry. Oh my, that was a long time ago.

Lights fade on Old Bride and Young Bride appears.

YOUNG BRIDE Growing up in Gooseberry I made friends with Rose McGrath from Patrick's Cove. Oh, we became great friends. Now Rose, later on, she married Allan. Anyway I used to love to go over to Patrick's Cove on the weekends to see Rose and I'd often stay over on Saturday night and come home on Sunday. So it was over there that I met this young fellow by the name of Patsy Judge. He lived there in Patrick's Cove, but he wasn't born there. He originally came from Gull Cove. His mother died when he was only six weeks old and so Thomas McGrath and Min, Min Tremlett, she was from Cuslett, took him and raised him. Patsy's own father took sick and moved to Cuslett with his brother Jerry, and that's where he died in 1927. Patsy was only fifteen years old when his father died. So the two of us were orphans, you might say. We were both raised by people other than our parents. So, anyway, myself and Patsy met then and we … well, you know … we took a liking to one another and we started courtin'… I suppose you'd call it. But he almost didn't get me and it was his own fault too. He was walking to Gooseberry to see me and we were supposed to meet in a certain place when he made a detour to go into Stoneyhouse.

Lights fade and come up on Patsy walking along the road. He stops and sits down and sings "Get Away, Old Man, Get Away." While he sings, Young Bride sits on the other side of the stage waiting with her arms folded across her chest. When Patsy finishes the song, he lies down on the ground.

PATSY I'll lie down here now a spell and wait for Bride. I'll just curl up and rest for a small bit.

Young Bride paces back and forth and stops on the road.

YOUNG BRIDE So he got in among the alders and he lay down and he fell asleep. And I stayed there by the road and stood up there for two or three hours. Oh, I got some mad. I stormed off back home. And so he went and he thought I was after leaving him. We got the place mixed up. There was no phone to call or nothing. He come over the next evening and I never spoke to him. Oh, I wasn't mad then. No, see, I thought he was after leavin' me. Oh, we couldn't get nothing straight. *(Laughs)*

YOUNG BRIDE Anyhow, we patched it all up. They says we were a good-looking couple. Now I'm not braggin', that's only what they says. I knew he was handsome. I knew that from the first time I saw him. He had the sweetest face and clear blue eyes and what a block of a man he was. Terrible broad shoulders and erect. Just like that he was. Oh yes, a handsome man. And lots of women thought that. In around Placentia and everywhere.

Young Bride exits and a woman enters.

WOMAN #1 Mary, come here. There he goes. Look, Mary! *(Looks through curtains)*

Another woman enters and joins her at the window.

WOMAN #2 What? Who? Where? What are you talking about?

WOMAN #1 Patsy Judge, girl! There he goes up the road. Look, oh my, he's a sight for sore eyes!

WOMAN #2 Oh yes, now I sees him. Oh yes, he's some nice and tall and look at the posture on him. Nice head of hair too. What's his name? Where's he from?

WOMAN #1 He's Patsy Judge, girl, I told you. He's from the Cape Shore, sure. All the handsome men comes from out there. *(Sighs)*

WOMAN #2 Go on now. You're only saying that because you comes from out there.

WOMAN #1 Because I comes from out there and because

it's the truth. Sure, Patsy is a prime example and he is the cream of the crop, I must say. And a fine singer too!

WOMAN #2 He sings too? Oh my, and do he dance?

WOMAN #1 Oh, he dances and he plays the tin whistle too.

WOMAN #2 And the tin whistle! Oh my.

WOMAN #1 And the fife.

WOMAN #2 And the fife! What's the fife?

WOMAN #1 The fife? Well, I saw him play it one time over Christmas when me mammy used to go to Gooseberry. Tis like a flute, only it's made out of wood. It's played sideways like the flute. They say he got it from Dick English, a man from St. Bride's who had a tilt over in Red Head. Now I don't know … I'm only telling you what was toldt to me. Anyhow, they say he also learnt it from Mr. James Joe Doyle in Gooseberry. The man who reared Bride, his wife.

WOMAN #2 *(In a sad voice)* His wife? He's married?

WOMAN #1 Married, yes. And Bride is shockin' jealous, so give it up. *(Elbows Woman #2)* They say that the fife come all the way from Ireland when one of the first settlers on the Shore came here.

WOMAN #2 Yes, yes. The fife. Too bad about the wife. *(Woman #1 elbows her again.)*

Both women sigh deeply looking out the window. Young woman exits; the other stays and becomes Old Bride.

OLD BRIDE Patsy always let stuff roll off him. He never minded anyone playing tricks on him or nothing like that. Oh, no. You could play tricks on Patsy all day long and he never cared, and he never cared about you laughin' at him.

You see, the thing is, Patsy'd always have the last laugh. Now there was this man here in the Cove who was good friends with Patsy. Anthony McGrath, and oh, Anthony could cod you all day long. Kind of what Leonard Manning is like. So when we left Gooseberry to come live in Patrick's Cove, him and Anthony'd go in the country together. They'd be in the country all day and there wouldn't be much to eat. The best thing you could bring in the country with you that time was lassy buns. So they had big brown lassy buns and they'd be boiling up in the night. A bad time come on them in country, you see, and they come out in Gooseberry. *(Old Bride puts on her pants and cap while talking.)* Now, Dick Dalton was living in Gooseberry that time too. Dick was also a Gooseberry man. There was only two houses in Gooseberry, see. So anyhow, they were all left Gooseberry and the stable was there ...

Old Bride becomes Anthony and Patsy enters. They sit down.

ANTHONY Patsy b'y, sure, we'll boil up now here behind the stable. We're gonna be tired when we gets home. It's dark now and that rain and snow'll keep blowin' in from the eastern. Jesus, Patsy, I'm soakin wet!

PATSY Yes, Anthony b'y, I'm soakin' wet meself. We puts ourselves through an awful lot for a few beavers. Yes, we do.

ANTHONY So we do, Patsy b'y. So we do.

PATSY We'll stay up here behind the stable now, Ton' b'y, till the wind dies down. Have you anything?

ANTHONY Oh yes, Patsy b'y, there's a couple of molasses buns there. We'll boil up the kettle now. I'll cut up the buns. *(Starts to cut the buns)* Some Jesus dark now, Patsy b'y.

PATSY Yes, Ton', it is. Mind your fingers now cuttin' up them buns. *(He fiddles with the fire.)* It's cold for November though, Ton', what?

ANTHONY Yes, Patsy b'y, it is cold. The buns is half
frozen.

*Anthony cuts the buns. Patsy watches and rubs his stomach
as he waits.*

ANTHONY You looks terrible hungry, Patsy.

PATSY Oh yes, and that's what I am. I'm starved, Tony
b'y. Give us a bun, Ton'. Give us a bun.

Anthony picks up a bun and hands it to Patsy.

PATSY I'll put a bit of butter on that.

*Patsy cuts the bun open, spreads butter on it and stuffs it in
his mouth. His eyes bulge out of his head. He spits it out and
jumps up.*

PATSY *(Laughs and slaps his leg)* Goddamn you, Tony.
Tis horse manure!

ANTHONY Patsy laughed about that till he died. Me
and Patsy used to sit in the rockin' chairs when we were
up in our seventies and we'd hit one another on the knees
laughing about that. Oh, Patsy had the ability to laugh at
anything. Another time Patsy got up one morning and
Patsy used to take all the young fellows in for a day
pickin' berries. They always used to go in the fall of the
year. Everyone had a half barrel out in the work house.
The half barrel of berries, you see, and you'd fill that with
berries and water and all the young fellows would think it
was a great thing for Patsy to take them in the country.
See Patsy was cute enough at gettin' them young fellows
to work for him. You see, he'd bring them in the country
and make them pick berries all day long, and see, he'd
sing songs, be tellin' them stories all day long. The young
fellows were having the time of their lives in the country
with Patsy. And he was as strong as an ox, so they'd pick
and he'd carry out the berries on his back. Oh, there'd be

ten or a dozen young fellows and you'd see them coming out of the country. You'd see them coming along and it was just like the time that fellow took the rats out of Hamburg. The Pied Piper, was it? Patsy in the lead with the berries on his back, singing away, and the line of young fellows following him. Oh my, it was some sight. That'd be something to see today now, wouldn't it? And the young fellows loved it. They didn't want the berries, no. They just wanted the fun of Patsy. The fun of Patsy singing. Now this time anyhow they were all crossin' the brook down there, you know, where Mike lives. That was the shortcut. They were crossing the brook and at that time they'd all stand up in the yard in the evening, you know, like on the corner in Branch, or down be Miller's in Placentia, the way people would stand around talking. So they used to stand up in the yard over there at the Y. There was a big flat rock and every man in the Cove used to go there in the evening and sit down on the rock and sing songs to pass the time.

Young Bride sings "Fair Fanny Moore" in the background. Patsy enters with a bag of berries on his back.

PATSY So I was coming along, crossing the brook with a bag of berries on my back and about ten or fifteen gallons in it. And Kevin over there, Kevin was full of devilment and he shouted out, roared out, "How you gettin' on, Patsy b'y?" And with that I spun around wavin' at Kevin. I spun around and dropped the bag of berries in the brook. The berries fell down the brook, they did. Dropped the berries in the brook, I got so flustered.

ANTHONY And that's the way he was. But no one was making fun of him, oh no. It wasn't that. He was too sweet a man to make fun of. No kind-hearted person was mean to him.

YOUNG BRIDE One time I was in to Miller's in Placentia, the store, you know, and I was looking for a new pair of men's pants for meself because, see, I wore the men's pants too. That was the time the shorts came out. You know, the short underwear. Before that we all had woolly bloomers. So anyhow everyone was buying the shorts, so I went into Miller's and bought four or five pairs. Spring came, and anyhow Patsy never wore 'em before. This time he took off the long johns and I said to him, I said, "I'm after buying you some shorts. You start wearing 'em now." "Yes, I will," he said to me. "Yes, I will." That's how he used to talk. "I'll wear them now, Bride." So he got up in the morning to go to work with the railway in Argentia, and Patsy never knew the difference in my bloomers and the shorts. So, what did he do, only haul on my bloomers. I didn't know. So he went off to work in Argentia with my bloomers on him. Uncle Dave Coffey down in Angel's Cove, he was there and he toldt us. He said Patsy went to go to the bathroom and Uncle Dave heard him cursing. "What's wrong, Patsy?" Dave asked. And Pasty said, "Ah Jesus, b'y," he said, "there's no fork in them shorts." Dave yelled out to him, "Ah God, there is, b'y, there must be!" "There's not," he yelled back. Dave said, "Come here till I have a look ... What's wrong with you, b'y?" he asked, but Dave knew, see, he was after seeing them sticking up in the back. "Look," Patsy said, "there's no fork." And Dave said, "How can there be, b'y? They're Bride's bloomers!"

ANTHONY Patsy was what you'd call an outfitter now, or a guide. He was some strong man. Oh my, just to give you an idea how strong Patsy was ... that time, there wouldn't be much grub going in the country. You'd have your fish and you'd have your potatoes that you'd bring in. And the St. John's fellows came out. Well, they weren't much good to walk. Well, I mean they weren't bad ... but they were St. John's men. They wouldn't be much good to work. But Patsy was just like a horse or a tractor that time. He'd take all the food. Some on a horse, some on a streel behind the horse and more on his back. So we were in there one day, in about two and a half hours. We were camped in the evening, we were camped there three or four days and we ran out of bread.

PATSY We got back to camp about three o'clock in the evening in the fall of the year. It's dark in the fall of the year at five o'clock and a two-and-a-half-hour walk. So anyhow, we were cuttin' wood down behind the camp and Tony said to me, "God, Patsy," he said, "I don't know what we're going to do with them goddamn St. John's fellows, b'y. We're out of grub. They'll kill us," he said. "We're gettin' paid, so what will we do?" he asked me. Well, I turned to him and I said, "Ton'," I said, "you stay and cut the wood and I'll run out and get the grub ... the bread, and they'll never know the difference."

ANTHONY So Patsy said to me, he said, "I'll run out and I'll get the bread and they'll never know the difference." "No!" I said. "You can't make it there and back again before it's dark! There's no sense in that!" Lord Jesus, I mean it would be humanly impossible! A humanly impossible feat! But off Patsy went. He left at three o'clock. Well, I was bringing the wood back to the camp and the St. John's fellows were there and every now and then they'd come and ask, "Where's Paddy Judge? Where's Paddy Judge?" And I'd say, "Oh, he's down there cuttin' wood." I'd be watchin' and Lord Jesus, I was sweatin' bullets too, I tell you. It got to settlin' in dark and I was wore out from lookin' and sweatin'. Then, by the Christ, didn't I see the lantern coming! And didn't I see Patsy runnin' and the steam comin' out of him! And with a whole load of bread in a flour sack on his back. And he wasn't gone three hours! And that a two-and-a-half-hour walk the one way!

PATSY Well, I left at three o'clock. Tony was against it. He kept sayin', "No, b'y Patsy, sure, you can't do that. It's an impossible thing and if you tries it, you could kill yourself tryin'," he said. So I thought it out. I knew it wouldn't be easy. But I took off and left Tony there at the wood and I made for it. I tore off and I kept meself movin'. I thought of every song I ever learnt. I went over and over them in me mind ... now I knows I sung this one while I was crossing the marsh.

Patsy sings "Uncle Dan McCann."

PATSY (*Finishes song*) ... So I cut out across the barrens and come into the Cove. Wasn't Bride surprised. And she just had the bread laid out and I said, "Bride, I got to take that now. I got to take that now and bring that into the camp with me." Sure, she thought I was cracked. She had no orders to make more bread for the camp. This was bread for the house and a bit extra, but I said, "Bride, I got to have that bread. I got to have that bread now, girl." Well, she was none too pleased, I can tell you. None too pleased and her bread disappearing like that. But she got me a flour sack none the less, and I and Bride started stackin' the bread into it. Now she wasn't getting paid for making the bread either, by the way, so Bride had double cause to be mad that day. And if the truth be known, well ... we weren't makin' anything off the whole endeavor ourselves. We were getting nothing. A few apples sometimes. Now, can you believe that? Well, tis true. A lot of them fellows, you know, they were miserable. And there's times they'd have us wash their backs ... and their feet. People don't know the half of it. Tony used to curse them. Oh, he cursed them into the clouds. But anyway ... where was I? Yes, oh yes ... so I come runnin' back in over the barrens, runnin' and runnin' I was, so we wouldn't get in trouble. I kept thinkin' on Tony being in there having to make up stuff to the St. John's fellows. I didn't want him to get anxious, so

I took a lantern from home and lit it when it drew on dark. I didn't want to go down into a bog hole, after all me trouble either, see. So I saw the camp and I headed for it. And, oh my, I was sweatin'! Well I wasn't even sweatin' when I got there. No sir, I was steamin'! The steam was rising off me. I suppose Tony thought I was a spirit with the way the vapor was risin' off me! But I made it. Yes sir! I made it back in time and the other fellows, well, they never knew the difference.

ANTHONY Yes, he made it. "The gunners," we called them fellows from town. But they gunned nothing. We had to kill the birds for them. They couldn't hit the side of a house. We had to kill the birds for them. That's the truth. What we should have been doin', we should have sold 'em the birds, is what we should have done. Never mind givin' 'em to them. We caught on after a while. But it took us a long time. I'll say that. We took a keen disliken' to them for the way we was treated 'cause there wasn't many nice men among 'em. It was in 'em to be miserable, I suppose.

PASTY One time I took an oven in on me back. Yes, an oven! You knows … a Waterloo. Some of 'em were round, but the Waterloo, he wasn't, he was square. He used to open from both ends, the oven from a Waterloo. And that's what we used to use for the stoves. They were made out of heavy iron and I'd haul it in on me back. I suppose I was a slave, you'd say, if there was ever a slave. I never cared nothing about misery, like I toldt you. This is what I was good at, I mean what I knew. They called me a … what do you call it now … one of them fellows up in Labrador somewhere. Oh, I knows I was never no good to fence or anything like that. That's not the kind of thing that interested me, see. No, I liked trappin' and I loved the country. I believe I could tell you anything about the country. Yes sir. I believe I could. Now, I mean, there were men that could have known more, I'm not saying that, but I did love the country. I was interested in that, you see, I had a liking for it and I followed my liking, so to speak.

ANTHONY Patsy used to work down in Argentia with the railway and never paid five cents transportation. He come in and the fellows on the boat'd bring him out, and my young fellows were fellows with cars and Patsy'd persuade them to bring him in. Patsy'd sing the whole ways in the Shore, that's the truth. Patsy'd get in and sing to them. He'd say to them, "My God, you're a grand young fellow, you are. By God, you'll get the girls in Placentia tonight." And then Patsy'd sing. Coddin' them, see? They were proper delighted. Patsy coddin' them the whole time. They didn't care. They'd drop him off. How often did one of my young fellows bring Patsy to Argentia like that. Patsy'd go singing for them when they'd be down there in the night. Patsy'd say, "What are you going at tomorrow, young fellow?" And they'd say, "We don't know, b'y, we might go to Placentia for a drive." And Patsy'd say, "You will, you will, you will! By God, you'll go into Placentia and I'll go in with you." And they'd have to bring him in then.

Young Bride and Patsy sing "Paper and Pins."

OLD BRIDE Well, one time meself and Patsy'd be all the rage for singing. "Bride," they'd say, "sing us a song, Bride," and I would. And Patsy could play the tin whistle too, see. And the fife. We had that fife for a long spell. It was Dick English's fife that Patsy had. He's the man that made the tune, the spirit tune. We used to store it in the pickle barrel to keep it plemmed so it wouldn't dry out. And one time I forgot it was in there and I broke it rootin' around. That was too bad because that was an old antique, that was. But Patsy used to play the whistle a lot, the tin whistle. And he learnt how to play the spirit tune on the whistle. He learnt it from old Mr. Gerald Foley who was the only person had that tune at that time. Patsy was only about eighteen then and Gerald Foley was about sixty. At that time an awful lot of people really believed in spirits. Now this ole Dick English, the way he toldt it, he had a tilt down there in Red Head. He'd go down there and wherever he went he had his old fife. When he was going to bed, he put the fife up on two nails. And when he was almost asleep he thought he heard the door swing and the next thing he thought he heard was the fife rattling. The next thing this fellow started to play the fife ... Dick could see nobody and he played a tune.

Patsy enters playing the tune.

OLD BRIDE And when he had it finished, Dick heard him take the fife and put it back up on the nail again and he heard him close the door, and then he said he picked up the fife and played the tune himself. Nobody in the area at that time had ever heard the tune before. We played at the folk festivals in town, and up in Ontario. Oh, we played everywhere. In 1975 we travelled up to Ottawa with the Wareham Brothers. The last night we were there, they gave a Newfoundland Soiree out there on the Rideau Canal. They advertised it in the paper and they advertised it on the radio, and they said they checked in about five hundred Newfoundlanders that night. That place was blocked ... you couldn't move! When it came to my turn to sing we edged up through the crowd, and when we left to get back to our seats I couldn't get through the crowd, so they took me, body and bones, took me right in their arms and passed me along and laid me down by the table. Then they said, "Mrs. Judge, next year you can get a first-class ticket up here if you want to come." They really enjoyed it. And the crowd down here enjoyed it too, you know, when we played for all the garden parties. Sometimes Patsy'd get so tired, after playing into the whistle all night long, he'd get so short-breathed blowing into the whistle all night long that I'd get up and go over and stand behind him and I used to blow into it for him. Yes, I did. This is how we'd manage it.

Old Bride gets up, goes over behind Patsy's chair and blows into the whistle that Patsy is holding up on his shoulder.

OLD BRIDE That's what we did because the people didn't want us to stop, and we didn't want to disappoint them. Oh, we had people from all over interested in the music. Ryan's Fancy came out and Kenny Goldstein from the university, and Pamela Morgan, Noel Dinn and them, and Aidan O'Hara from Ireland. They made tapes and movies. Aidan wanted to take us to Ireland and he had the tickets and all, but then the troubles broke out again over there and we couldn't go. Aidan used to say we were more Irish than the Irish back in Ireland. He'd say it was because of how the Cape Shore was cut off for so long. I suppose he could be right. The old ways were all we knew. Everything we knew was passed down from the old people. You take the old songs now, they all had verses like poetry. They toldt something from beginning to end. Not like the ones you hear now, where you wonder where they originated from. But all them old songs, they were made about something that actually happened. Some were sad. Some were delightful. Whatever happened, they made a song to suit it.

Young Bride sings "Katie O'Ryan."

PATSY I was cookee down on the base, the American base in Argentia. They used to call me cook, but sure, I wasn't able to boil water. No, I wasn't. They called me cook anyway, but I was able to laugh at that because I was eatin', wasn't I? Anyway, this one night the head fellow from the railway was there and I had to bring him his soup. *(Acts it out)* So anyway, I brought him out the bowl and I had it chock full, see, and well … I had me two thumbs down in the soup to make it easy to carry. I was holding it like that. "Here's your soup, Skipper," I says. "Here's your soup." Then Skipper says, "By God, Paddy, you have all right, but you have your two thumbs in it. You have your two thumbs down in me soup." And I says to him, "Ah, that's the best kind, Skipper, sure, that's not hot. I'm not burned the one bit," I says to him. And I shoved it over to him like that.

OLD BRIDE Patsy never had to wash his face in his life. He didn't. But in five minutes he'd be ready to get up and sing. He could rig up and go on stage. That kind of stuff didn't bother Patsy. He was a unique man and handsome. You should have seen him when he was dressed up, the ole bones of him. But, you know, he wasn't as good on stage in Bannerman Park as he was sittin' down here next to me singing.

Patsy sings "Bonny Bunch of Roses O."

PATSY One time Tony had the flu ... the time he was fishing and it was the first capelin and he was in bed for a whole week. We were all telling him to get a bottle of rum and burn it out him. And he said, "If I could get rum with liniment, I'd burn it out of me." So Piercy came out that time. Piercy was the peddler who come out once every two weeks. He had the rum with him. So Tony bought the rum and mixed it up with Sloane's Minors Liniment. Mixed it up in a glass, said he'd burn the flu out of him. At that time there was no running water. That time it run from the spring well, you know, where Dominic lives. Ton' mixed it up in the glass and downed it like that and when he downed it ... ahhhh *(Makes raspy sound)* his throat went and he ran to the buckets and the buckets were empty. And there was no tap. And he ran, and Ton' never went through the door a day in his life without his head covered because he was bald, see. So he rushed for the cap and he jumped the gate like a foal and ran and shook his head under the water, and ten minutes after, his breath came back. He burnt the whole lining out of his throat. He was the whole summer and never spoke. Burnt it out.

YOUNG BRIDE James Joe Doyle, that's who Patsy went to school to, what we call it. What education Patsy had, he got it from Mr. Doyle and he was also a smart man. He wasn't a worker as such, like to go at something. James Joe wasn't going building a boat. He'd sing and get someone else to build the boat. He'd get a bunch of young fellows from over here to Gooseberry and he'd go up in the woods and he'd play the whistle and they'd cut wood. And he'd sit up on the ridge and he'd tell stories all day and tell them about the fine girls in around Placentia. And they proper delighted, thinkin' they were going to get them too. And that's where Patsy got all his ... people would say, Patsy, you're the real James Joe.

OLD BRIDE They'd all get nicknames. James Joe was Bras. That could be his father or his grandfather he got the nickname off of. Like Tramore ... now the first time I heard tell of Tramore was the time an old man died here. Someone at the wake said, "Well, here comes Tramore blessin' the corpse." Tramore was Thomas Foley from Little Barasway. His offspring are over there yet. Tommy and Jimmy ... all them fellows were terrible smart men. Couldn't read or write, but, oh my, the things they could do. But you know there was never a Sunday that there wasn't a crowd to our place. And not all local people. No, people from everywhere. Priests and bishops, royalty and the poor humble fishermen. All were welcome to Bride and Patsy Judge's. Yes sir. You often hear the saying, "Play the flute and play the harp depending on where I was." Well, Patsy could play the flute or play the harp, so to speak. He could dance to anyone's tune, Patsy could. And argue. Patsy could sit down and argue till daylight, and then get up and go home. You couldn't vex him.

YOUNG BRIDE If we got a call from anywhere in the Cove and were toldt that someone was there with a guitar or something then, by the God, Patsy'd wipe the cloth across his face and say, "Come on now, Bride, we'll go over"... to such and such a house. Oh, we wouldn't be long going. No sir. Now it wouldn't be all music and singing. No, we'd talk about everything under the sun for a couple of hours. And then someone'd say, "By God, Patsy, I think you'll try one." And then he'd take off his overshoes, and then he'd take off his coat ... and the party was on then. Fast step, the party was on. Oh, there wasn't much drinking now. No, maybe Patsy'd take two drinks while we were all talking. Youngsters'd be peeping around laughing. The party was on then. Patsy'd say, "Did you ever hear this one?" And he'd tell you the story of it. Where he got and all that.

Patsy sings "Prisoner of Newfoundland."

PATSY The truth be known I never liked fishing; 1938 was the last year I fished. We didn't get very much for the fish and we brought it into Placentia and sold it, believe it or not, at that time for $2.50 a quintal. So the first chance I could get, I was getting clear of that. I never went back at that for a living. I was fed up on that. But, you know, some called me an entertainer and I suppose I was that. All I know is I like the old songs, and the old tunes. I like them more than anything. It's a pity that a lot of them were forgotten. They'll never be revived again because an awful lot of people that have them, like myself, are getting old now, and the young people have the new stuff coming in. I suppose everything has its day. But it took a lot of thinking to make those old songs. I don't think there is any poet could improve on the poetry that's in them. And the old people could sing them as well as anybody you could hear today. You know the best thing to come out of all our going around, I and Bride, the best thing was bringing all the people together. People from all over the island could hear us and we could get a chance to hear their songs, see. And if you spreads it around like that, maybe it won't be lost. Maybe ... I hope not anyway. It would be a shame to lose what all the old people knew. It would, wouldn't it?

OLD BRIDE So much has changed. The times ... we've had a full life. I'm not complaining. We raised a house full of youngsters, two of our own and ten foster children. Patsy is gone now. He got weak-minded later on. I'm not all that good meself some days. But his mind'd wander and sometimes he'd wander off himself. Kinda like he was tryin' to follow something in his mind. He passed away into the Miller Centre. I didn't want him to go. I wanted to take care of him meself, but I come to realize I couldn't at the end of it. There'll never be another man like my Patsy. Oh no. He was a man you don't meet everyday, I can tell you that. A Cape Shore man. An Irishman you could say. A gentleman through and through. If I had one wish for everyone in the world, for the young people comin' up today, you know what that wish would be? That they could run into a man like my Patsy. Yes, then the world would be a richer place, now, wouldn't it? Yes, I do believe it would.

Young Bride and Patsy sing "The Blooming Bright Star of Belle Isle."

An audio recording of *A Man You Don't Meet Everyday* can be found on the Alder Institute website (www.alder.nf.ca), Audio Archive. Episode 82.

JUST ASK ROSIE

Approximately 40 minutes

Just Ask Rosie was first produced in 2003 at the Cuslett Community Arts Centre. *Just Ask Rosie* incorporates parts of the play *Answer Me Home* written by Agnes Walsh and Paul Rowe.

Two elderly close friends meet several times a week for a chat. Neither has ever married and so each depends on the other for company and the keeping alive of stories from their communities. A young woman befriends them both and her interest in their stories and songs only enlivens their get-togethers. The settlement history of the Cape Shore, as well as many other stories from the oral tradition, enrich this play.

LIST OF CHARACTERS & ACTORS (2003 PRODUCTION)

ROSIE: Mildred Dohey
JOHNNY: Christopher Young
MARY ANNE: Kay Coffey

ROSIE *(Enters and straightens up a picture)* Me picture is all gone sideways. What happened to it, I wonder?

Johnny is sitting in the audience. He sings two verses of a song while Rosie sets the table. She puts some wood in the stove and fills up the kettle.

JOHNNY I must make a dart over to Rosie's. *(Gets up, goes to the door, fixes his hair and tugs his pants from his rear-end.)*

ROSIE *(Sweeps the floor until she hears a knock. She checks her slip, peeps in the mirror and fixes herself.)* Oh, it's himself, is it?

ROSIE *(Opens the door)* Good evening, Johnny. The fine weather brought you out. Come in.

JOHNNY Good evening yourself, Rosie. It's a fine evening all right.

ROSIE I was just taking a cup of tea and a lemon crème, Johnny. Would you like to join me?

JOHNNY Don't mind if I do here, now, Rosie. Your lemon crèmes were always the best in the Cove.

Rosie shows a box to the audience and smiles, while Johnny seats himself.

ROSIE I'm having a visitor today so you'd better be on your best behaviour.

JOHNNY A visitor? You mean a stranger?

ROSIE Well, no. I knows her, but she's coming on a bit of a formal visit to interview me.

JOHNNY To interview you? You mean for the television?

ROSIE No, no, with a microphone and a recorder or

something. She's a writer, b'y. She's terrible interested in the history of the Shore.

JOHNNY The history of the Shore? Is she coming to interview you ... or me?

ROSIE Oh, so you're the expert on the Shore now, are you, Mr. Johnny? You knows it all, I expect. Yet it's me she's after ... not yourself.

JOHNNY Now, Rosie, you know as much as I do, just different that's all.

There's a knock on the door.

ROSIE That'd be her.

JOHNNY It's Grand Central Station here tonight!

ROSIE *(At the door)* Mary Anne, come on in, Mary Anne.

MARY ANNE Good evening, Rosie.

ROSIE This here is Johnny Cleary from up the road. Johnny, this is Mary Anne McHugh from up the Shore.

JOHNNY *(Gets up slowly and shakes her hand)* Pleased to meet you, my dear.

MARY ANNE Good evening, Johnny, so good to finally meet you.

ROSIE Come on, Mary Anne. Come over and have a cup of tea.

JOHNNY Rosie was just serving me a cup of tea. I suppose she'll offer you a bickie too.

MARY ANNE *(Sits down)* A cup of tea would be grand. My, but it's some sweltering warm out there. They say that drinking hot tea is the best thing for you in the heat. Do you think that's true?

ROSIE Hot tea is good for anything, my dear. Anything that ails ya and it stimulates the brain. I read that in the *Reader's Digest*.

JOHNNY Hot tea! A drop of rum is what stimulates the brain, Rosie girl. You must have read that wrong.

ROSIE You lay off that ole rum talk. This woman is here on serious business now.

MARY ANNE *(Reaches for her bag and takes out a recorder)* Oh, just for a chat really, and if you don't mind me recording our chat?

ROSIE No, go on, girl.

JOHNNY Rosie here tells me you're interested in the history of the Shore.

MARY ANNE *(Puts a tape in and presses play)* That's right, sir, I am. I like to record the history and write plays about it.

ROSIE There you go now, Johnny! You want to be in one of Mary Anne's plays? You're the actor, sure, you are.

JOHNNY Now, Rosie girl, I used to entertain in me day, that's for sure, at the concerts and all that. I liked the old stories. Now Rosie here is a good hand at the stories, miss.

MARY ANNE Yes, I know that. The last time I was out I wore out two tapes!

JOHNNY Did she tell you about the first settlers on the Shore?

MARY ANNE The first settlers? No, we talked about midwives, the war and stuff like that.

ROSIE Oh, let him tell you about the first people here

then, Mary Anne. He likes to go way back. He may look ninety, but he's got the brain of a two-hundred-year-old.

JOHNNY Now, Rosie girl, you watch yourself now. Neither one of us are spring chickens. But see, I used to love hearing the stories from the old people. I used to hide under the kitchen table listening and I never forgot them.

MARY ANNE Who were the first settlers here? The Irish, I suppose?

JOHNNY Well, the first settlers were planters that Sweetman and Saunders brought over here to fish and to farm. And some of them were running from something.

MARY ANNE Running from something?

JOHNNY Well, yes, like the 1798 Rebellion. You heard tell of that? The Catholics were making a stand against the landlords, the gentry. They were the poor farmers who couldn't own a bit of land. They could only rent off the landlords. And these gentry, they lived like kings off the backs of the poor Irish. Well, some stood up to them and then they had to flee. I'd say Sweetman hid a few aboard his boats because rumour had it he was on the side of the United Irishmen in the 1798 Rebellion.

ROSIE But, Johnny, it was said that the first settler in Patrick's Cove was on the run for killing his stepmother.

JOHNNY Old Bartley. That's what the old people used to say. That he was from Tipperary and he got in a row with her and stabbed her with a pitchfork and flung her over the hedge. Now, I don't know if it's true or not, but either way, he would have boarded a boat in Waterford, a boat belonging to Sweetman, who was the merchant in Placentia. And he would have hid out here in the marsh or the woods. All that crowd who came over married women from different parts of the Shore, I suppose.

ROSIE For God's sake, Johnny, that was years ago. She's not interested in all that.

MARY ANNE No, no, I am, anything to do with the Shore. John Mannion from the university said that all the Irish who came to Newfoundland came from within a thirty-mile radius of Waterford.

JOHNNY Thirty miles! That's a small pool of blood! What does that say, I wonder?

MARY ANNE Well, sir, I don't know, but I heard that Placentia Bay had some load of talent come out of it. I mean there's Ray Guy, Anita Best, Rex Murphy, Baxter Wareham, Al Pittman, Pat and Joe Byrne, Mercedes Barry, Eddie Coffey and the list goes on and on!

JOHNNY Are you saying that we're all cracked or that we're all geniuses?

MARY ANNE Well, sir, a fine line there could be between the two ... a fine line.

ROSIE That's enough debate over madness and smartness. Tell the girl something useful, for God's sake, Johnny.

JOHNNY Useful? Now, I don't know about useful, but I'll tell you about the twenty-seven years I spent fishin'.

MARY ANNE Where did you fish, sir?

JOHNNY Off here and everywhere. The Perch, the Cape, the Shoal. I went fishing when I was only thirteen. The first year, I didn't go with me father. I went with another man here from St. Bride's, Jack Murphy, from up on the hill.

ROSIE Margaret Morrissey's grandfather.

JOHNNY Yeah, Margaret Morrissey's grandfather.

Jack's father came over from Ireland, we think. We think he was the last one to come over from Ireland. I liked fishing. I had to leave school when I was only thirteen for one reason. Me father got sick that spring and he wasn't able to go fishing. Back then, it would be useless to go to a merchant to get supplies for fishing if you weren't in your health and strength. They'd only laugh at you, so I had to take up the job. At that time, there was what you'd call a government guarantee given.

ROSIE Oh yeah, that was up there on the corner.

JOHNNY Yeah, up there on the corner. There were a couple of fellows out from St. John's. You'd get a bit of supplies to go fishin' like …

ROSIE Salt …

JOHNNY Rubber boots, jiggers and lines. Anyway, I wrote my list and I went to them. They turned me down … too young.

ROSIE Tut, tut.

JOHNNY They wouldn't give it to me, so I joined up with this old man in the end, Jack. "Ah," he said, "I'll get a bit of salt and we'll go fishing." So we got the salt from the merchant up here. You know him, Rosie – Paddy Griffen.

ROSIE Gerald Griffen's father.

JOHNNY And we went at it. I'd go up every evening and say, "Will we get at it tomorrow, Jack?" "No, no," he says, "we'll go at it when the fish comes." He kept me like that for two weeks before we'd go out. He didn't know. He just didn't want to be at it. Finally, he decided we'd go out. Anyway, we didn't do very good. I don't know what we got, thirty or forty quintals or something like that. Sure, Rosie, that was only small at that time … $2.50 or $3.00 a quintal.

ROSIE Nothing, nothing.

JOHNNY No, girl, nothing! So the next year me father got better and I went fishin' with him. He only had a row dory with a set of oars. You knows that, Rosie, we fished like that. Yes sir, we fished together for six or seven years before he died.

ROSIE Poor soul.

JOHNNY I use to have to join up with another fellow then. You'd do some goin' that time, what?

ROSIE Yeah, Johnny, yeah.

MARY ANNE And what about school, Johnny?

JOHNNY Oh no, you never learned nothin' about fishin' in school.

ROSIE No, b'y, she wants to know about the schools on the Shore, don't you, Mary Anne?

MARY ANNE Well I …

ROSIE Oh my, remember the teacher we had that time in Patrick's Cove? What was her name?

JOHNNY *(Laughs)* Remember, she'd get everyone in the Cove to stand up and give their full names.

ROSIE Yeah, she'd start with the boys. "Name please!" she'd call out. And they'd say, "Patrick McGrath, miss." "Good," she'd say. "Next boy."

JOHNNY "Patrick McGrath, miss."

ROSIE "Two Patrick's," she'd say. "I see … well, I tell you what, I'll call you Patrick and you Pat. How's that? Problem solved. Next boy," she'd say.

JOHNNY "Patrick McGrath, miss."

ROSIE "Oh my, another ... well, will everyone here with the first name Patrick and the last name McGrath, please raise your hands." And she counted, one, two, three, four, five, and there'd be one fellow whose hand wasn't up.

JOHNNY Yeah, Tommy McGrath, and she'd ask him if he could help her out and he'd come up to the front of the class and point out who was who. He'd say, "He's Mike's Pat, and that there's John's Pat and he's Al's Pat," and so on.

ROSIE Remember the day she had to leave the classroom for a phone call and she put Tommy in charge of the class?

JOHNNY Oh Jesus, Mary and Joseph! Yes, and Albert took out his thing and started peeing over the whole class.

ROSIE Tut, tut, and poor Tommy got so nervous, and when she came back and asked him how it went and if everything was okay, Tommy said, "Well, miss, Albert had his squirter out and he was watering the whole class!"

JOHNNY And the teacher went over to Albert and she said ...

ROSIE *(Cuts in)* "Albert," she said, "you put that squirter right there in my hand!"

All hands laugh.

JOHNNY Oh blessed Jesus!

MARY ANNE Rosie, were there many recitations on the go when you were growing up?

ROSIE Recitations? Oh yes, you see, there was always concerts and you had older people who knew the old songs or stories or recitations.

JOHNNY Rosie, tell Mary Anne the one about the runaway bike. Now that's a recitation, my dear. No one else out here on the Shore has that one. Go on now, girl, tell it to her.

ROSIE Well now, Johnny, you're asking me for one now. I heard that this one came over from Cork, Ireland, and was made to suit the Shore here. I'll give it a go if you're ready.

MARY ANNE Oh yes, go right ahead, Rosie.

JOHNNY Go on now, girl, tell it to her. I'll go over and heave meself down in the rocking chair for a spell.

ROSIE *(Clears her throat)* I have to stand up to tell it 'cause it's easier to get out. It's called "The Runaway Bike."

Friends all the way beyond Branch and
from the Cape Shore Road
Wondered whether twas Paddy
worked out this wonderful plan
Or Biddy that mentioned it first to her man.
I'll tell you the tale as I heard it
And ye can judge for yourself who deserves all the credit.

They were sitting by the fire one night all alone
Reading The Charter and that one from *Downhome*
When Biddy read of a friar called Augustine
Who to glory had gone through spontaneous combustion.

Wisha, bless us, says Biddy, what can that be?
Hold on, says Pat, that's a thing that lights up by itself
without matches or sparks
Lights up by itself and goes off in the dark.

Now, says Biddy, with your motorbike
With its engine and plugs and points that won't spark
Get something spontaneous and don't break my heart.

Paddy was awful tough with the scheme
All day he would work and all night he would dream
With magnets and coils and spare pieces of tractor
He produced this machine of fierce interactor.

When all was complete being advised down to Wals
He decided to try her by Angel's Cove Falls
The fame of that bike having spread near and far
He was joined by his cousins from all over the shore.

Well they started to push, they started to nudge
They started to sweat, but that bike wouldn't budge,
By God, says Leonard Manning, she's a bad pill
Hold on, says Pat, once she'll start
she'll sweep up Ship Cove Hill.

Well the Doyles and the O'Keefes declared it was a dud
We've made up, says Pat, what the French call a fracas
Ship round to Tom Power for a loan of his jackass.

The donkey was brought, but he wasn't very frisky
What he needs, says Tom Power, is a good glass of whiskey
The whiskey was brought and Tom drank pretty quick
And then he persuaded the ass with a stick.

The donkey had gone but a couple of paces
When the bike gave a kick and it shot off both traces
And Pat had no time to jump on the seat
When the bike, like a bullet she flew up the street.

Oh the sight of the thing and the noise that it drove
It set every horse farting along Patrick's Cove
Oh the stink of that bike
when it approached Point La Haye
It knocked down a politician just in from Voisey's Bay.

There was mad Judy Mulligan at Manning's front door
She had read all the prophets from Job to old Moore
Tis the end of the world, she says, Babylon falls
And she ran like a hare for Peter and Paul's.

He almost near killed a boy at the Grotto
Hey! Get out you young brat you
Well he stepped on the pedal, and he pulled on the gasket
And before he knew it she was far into Cuslett.

For the further she went the more power she got
And Pat couldn't stop her if he were to be shot
At St. Bride's a friend of his shouted: Advance!
Before Pat could reply, she was into Point Lance.

The next place he saw was the great town of Branch
Who should he knock down but Gerald Campbell's mare
So they phoned on to Beckford to warn Tony Power
By the time he arrived she had only gained by the hour.

For North Harbour and Colinet he had
no trouble drawing near
And to save him the police tried to shoot him in Salmonier
His cap was shot off and his clothes were near gone
Ah shag it, Pat cried, I'll steer straight for St. John's.

With police in pursuit of each street that he passed
The fire brigade came out in full force
And when Pat came in sight they turned on the hose
What a chilly reception!
That's the townies for you, I suppose.

But with blood on the bumpers like hives on his ass
This machine never stopped
till she reached Port Aux Basques
And there for the blue pool, poor Pat felt her driving
His hair stood on his head 'cause he hated high diving.

When she rose in the air and she sunk in the waves
Poor Pat now he lies in some deep ocean cave
And his Biddy has given up hope

of finding him and the bike that he drove
So she took off and married a lad from Lear's Cove.

But the main mate of a submarine
Coming home from the West Indies
Swears one day while cleaning his windies
There passed him a bike looking messed up and busted
And the engine was stamped, "Manufactured in Cuslett."

MARY ANNE *(Claps)* What a recitation, Rosie! What a wonderful memory you have there!

ROSIE *(Bats her away with her hand)* Memory? I don't know about that … I suppose, but sure, Mary Anne, when I was growing up, all you had to rely on was your memory … your mind. Not like today with all the distractions of newspapers, television, radio, videos and computers. Oh my God Almighty, it's a wonder the young people have a mind to call their own. Take my friend Johnny there, when we get together for a visit, do we talk about what's on television?

JOHNNY No.

ROSIE No, what do we talk about, Johnny? Tell her!

MARY ANNE What do you talk about on an evening, Johnny?

JOHNNY *(Grins to himself)* Well …

ROSIE *(Cuts in)* We talks about life, real life, the past or what's going on now, not the gossip. Although there might be a bit of that, but we goes over what happened mostly, like now, the other evening Johnny was here and we were talking about the road, the Cape Shore road.

MARY ANNE The Cape Shore road? Well that must have been a hard ole road at one time, if it was a road at all then.

ROSIE *(Laughs)* And that's what it was, a hard ole road. Remember, Johnny, the time that surveyor come out from St. John's, and he brought a cow with him and whatever way the cow turned that's where they put the road.

JOHNNY *(Laughs)* Yes, and remember, Rosie, old Magistrate Sinnott brung out the first car to the shore, or that's the way I heard it. He used to have to get out and push the car up Gooseberry Hill.

MARY ANNE Stop it now, I know you're joking. But what if you met another car on the road? It must have been so narrow that the alder bushes would be scraping against the windows. There couldn't have been any room to pass.

ROSIE One or the other would have to back up till you came to a wide place. Remember, Johnny, Jim Verran was going up Ship Cove Hill one time and he sees a light coming, so he said to himself, "I'm in a nice wide place here, I'll pull over and wait here now for the fellow to pass." Well, he waits and he waits and he waits and no sign of a car, so he carries on up the hill slowly, till he sees it was just the light from the moon.

MARY ANNE The moon?

ROSIE It was the full moon rising in the sky.

MARY ANNE Where was that again?

ROSIE Ship Cove, on Coach's Puzzle. I bet you don't know where that's to.

MARY ANNE No, I never heard of it.

JOHNNY Well, Grandfather said that part of the road was designed by an engineer from St. John's named Coach. It came down the side of the hill like a "Z" and more than one fellow got out of his car halfway down

Coach's Puzzle and walked to the bottom thinking he'd lost his way. Coach said he had to make it into an "S" and some fellow said to him, "Boy, you'd be better off to make it into an 'O.'"

ROSIE And, Johnny, do you remember Thomas Palfrey from Placentia?

JOHNNY Jesus, yes, girl.

ROSIE He was trying to get up this side of Big Barsway. Well, he tried three times to get up that one winter with a crowd of fellas aboard. No sir, he couldn't do it. So he told them to get out and he backed halfway through Barsway and gave her a run for it. He almost made it to the top, but he lost control and she went over the side and into the woods. Palfrey, he was a nice ole fella, never got upsot, he was always the one mood. He climbs out of her and he looks at the car and he looks at the fellas and says, "Jesus, b'y, what a grand time to put a muffler on her."

All hands laugh.

JOHNNY Oh, Jesus, Mary and Joseph!

MARY ANNE Ahhh … neither of you never married. How come?

ROSIE Well, Johnny here was too busy having a good time. Singing and going around being opinionated.

JOHNNY And you were too proud.

ROSIE *(Folds her arms across her chest)* I am not proud!

JOHNNY Too fond of your own company.

ROSIE And what's wrong with being able to get along with yourself and being independent?

JOHNNY Oh nothing, Rosie girl, but you certainly always made a point of it.

ROSIE *(Put out)* Humph! Oh for God's sake, Johnny b'y, sing us one of your gallivanting songs to change the topic.

JOHNNY See, Mary Anne, she was always like that. Change the topic. You're cute enough, Rosie. I'll sing this one for you, Mary Anne.

Johnny sings "Ninety Years Old."

MARY ANNE Good job, Johnny!

JOHNNY See, I sang in the concerts when Father Lawler was here. He was a concert man, a real concert man. That was in the ... before the eighties.

ROSIE Yeah, the sixties.

JOHNNY Yeah, he was here in the sixties, I think.

MARY ANNE *(Looks at each of them sweetly)* And the two of you never courted ... like ... you know.

ROSIE *(Gets flustered)* Courted? Well, no. I mean we were always the best of friends, weren't we?

JOHNNY I think the girl is askin' how come the two of us never married, but sure, Lord Jesus, girl, I'd never afford to send you to Bingo.

Johnny hits the table and laughs.

ROSIE Oh, go away with yourself. Mary Anne, Johnny here was too busy having a good time singing and going around and his mouth on the bottle.

JOHNNY Now, what's wrong with havin' a drink? See, Rosie never puts a drop to her lips, see.

ROSIE I don't need it. I can have me opinion. I can talk and tell a tale or two. I can tell you anything at all, and I don't need a drink to back me up.

JOHNNY *(Tenderly)* That's right. She's right. If there's anything at all, Mary Anne, that you wants to know just ask Rosie. That's true.

MARY ANNE Did you ever want to go to Ireland, Johnny?

JOHNNY Oh, girl, I suppose I'd go if I had lots of money.

ROSIE He don't need to go. All Ireland is up here in his head. Sing her an Irish song, Johnny, for God's sake.

JOHNNY I could, I could sing "County Mayo." Ever hear that one?

MARY ANNE No.

ROSIE Yes, that's an old Irish song.

Johnny sings "County Mayo."

MARY ANNE Well done, Johnny!

JOHNNY Now, my dear, you should have met Thomas Murphy. He was a real Irishman, sounded like one. Sang like one too. Fellows from Ireland used to be up to Thomas' all the time. His wife was Minnie.

Rosie sings "Tom Tobin's Dickey Bird."

JOHNNY Nicky was Thomas' brother.

MARY ANNE Oh yeah, and what about shipwrecks along the coast?

JOHNNY Do you know about Joe Careen and the crowd that were in jail that time over the boat, the *Maude Best*?

MARY ANNE No.

ROSIE She was a mystery.

JOHNNY She was the mystery of all mysteries happened to her. She passed out here St. Stephen's Day, I believe, jogging out the bay. She went out the bay that evening at three or four o'clock with a little draft of a northerly wind. She was off here at St. Bride's about four o'clock the next morning, and the next morning she was high and dry in Lear's Cove. The weather that night in question, the wind veered out of the southeast, or the easterly, there was a living gale and snowin'. But she should have been well over in St. Mary's Bay whatever happened. But anyway, there was a dance down in the hall in St. Bride's, and meself and me friend, we went outside to take a breath. We looked up and the light was out on Cape St. Mary's. My friend said, "Be Golly, they're gone to bed early on the Cape tonight!" The next morning, the *Maude Best* was high and dry in Lear's Cove. The light on the Cape should have been on, it should have been flashing. Perhaps they fell asleep and they never welled her up. You'd have to wind up the light, whoever was out there. And in the cabin was a deck of cards on the table and there was plates and cups and saucers not stirred. Now that was a mystery. She had fish, dried fish. She was going to St. John's. And cod oil, whatever, her summer earnings, whatever they got. My opinion about it ... she had to run down the Bulls coming back when she struck the gale in St. Mary's Bay. They turned back, that's what I think, they had to turn back to be on this side of the Cape. The wind veered in from the wester that night, that morning. She had to run down the Bulls or run down the Cape 'cause twas snowing and a living gale. That's all I could make of it. And no one aboard and nothing stirred. They were never seen or heard tell of since. They were from Clarke's Beach down in Conception Bay. They all went to jail on the head of her. Oh, Joe Careen could have toldt you the story about her, yes sir! Yes, and Joe Careen could have told you lots more too. But sure, Rosie here got the whole story, don't ya, Rosie? Just ask Rosie, Mary Anne.

ROSIE Just ask Rosie. Just ask Rosie. You only wants me to talk so you can get your mouth back on the bottle. Don't think I don't know you got one.

JOHNNY *(Sheepishly)* It's only a small one, Rosie.

MARY ANNE Will you tell me the whole story, Rosie?

ROSIE Well, I'll tell it to you, Mary Anne. I'll tell it too as if Joe Careen was telling it to ya!

Rosie tells Joe Careen's story. (See To the City of Point Lance*)*

ROSIE Now, Mary Anne, that's the way Joe Careen toldt it to me.

MARY ANNE My God, Rosie, that was some good story. They certainly had it hard them times.

ROSIE Yes, girl, they did, but them times are gone now. That would never happen today … Well, never mind that now.

JOHNNY I'll give another song now before I goes home, a special one, a special one for you, Rosie. Come on, Rosie, let's dance.

ROSIE No …

JOHNNY Come on …

ROSIE No …

JOHNNY Come on …

ROSIE No …

MARY ANNE Go on, Rosie girl.

JOHNNY Come on …

ROSIE Oh, all right.

Rosie and Johnny dance, while Johnny sings "Just Ask Rosie."

ROSIE *(Stops dancing)* Now knock it off, Johnny b'y, it's getting late and I'm beat out with all the goings on.

JOHNNY *(Puts away flask)* Yes, Rosie girl, it's time for me to head home now.

MARY ANNE *(Gets up and packs away her recorder)* Hang on there, Mr. Johnny, I'll give you a run over to your place now. I'll take you home.

JOHNNY Did you hear that, Rosie? I'm being escorted home by this beautiful young woman. Are ya jealous yet?

Rosie pulls Mary Anne close before she leaves.

ROSIE Men! Nothing but big babies, and the older they get the more attention they needs.

MARY ANNE I suppose, girl!

ROSIE *(Goes over to Johnny, moves close to his face and cups his chin with her hand)* I'll see you tomorrow evening, Johnny, and we'll get down to more SERIOUS business … a good game of cards.

ROSIE *(Smacks Johnny's cheek and looks at Mary Anne)* Good night, Mary Anne. Stop by and see me any time.

MARY ANNE Good night, Rosie. It was wonderful seeing you again. Come on, Mr. Johnny.

Johnny and Mary Anne exit through side door. Rosie clears the table, hums to herself and sits down.

ROSIE Men! Well, he's a good friend, Johnny is, and how many years has it been? That says a lot in itself.

Light goes off Rosie. Johnny and Mary Anne walk off the stage and into audience.

JOHNNY She's a good woman, Rosie is. She got her head screwed on right, I'll tell ya. Stubborn though. Between you and me, Mary Anne, I would have married her years ago, but she was always too stubborn. Yeah, too stubborn, but I thinks the world of her, I do. Yes, I do.

CHASING CRIPPLE

Approximately 90 minutes

Chasing Cripple was first produced in 2005 at the Cuslett Community Arts Centre.

Set in modern times, *Chasing Cripple* tells the story of a middle-aged woman raising her family after the loss of her husband. Her mother lives with the family also. They take in a boarder who works for Parks Canada at Cape St. Mary's Bird Sanctuary. Issues arise over who has rights to shoot the seabirds that have traditionally been hunted on the Shore for centuries. Over a game of cards and during a dance at the local bar, many other issues such as family, dating and out-migration from rural Newfoundland are heatedly debated.

LIST OF CHARACTERS & ACTORS (2005 PRODUCTION)

ROSE (GRANDMOTHER): Mildred Dohey

LUCY (WIDOW): Kay Coffey

JUNIOR (SON): Bruce White

MARGIE (DAUGHTER): Erin McGrath

LILY (WILDLIFE OFFICER): Cheryl White

REG (SUITOR TO LUCY): John Cheeseman

BILLY (SUITOR TO LUCY): Christopher Young

BARTENDER: Wanda Coffey

An old woman is on her knees in the corner of the kitchen scrubbing, and singing "Sweet Forget Me Not" to herself.

GRANDMOTHER I don't know why they can't see the dirt. I'm half blind and I sees it. *(Throws rag aside and wipes her forehead)* There! The four corners are done at least. Four green fields. *(Sings "Four Green Fields" to herself)*

Door opens. A middle-aged woman enters and puts down two bags of groceries on the table. She looks across the room and sees the old woman on her knees.

LUCY Mother! For Jesus' sake, Mother! Get up off your knees! I'm after telling you there's no need for you to be doing that. You'll be crippled tomorrow, Mother. I can't turn me back on you! *(Moves toward her mother and tries to help her up)*

GRANDMOTHER *(Swipes her away with her arm)* Leave me alone! If I got down here, I can get back up. Back off! Go! Get! *(She struggles, but manages to get up on her own.)*

LUCY Mother, there's no need for you to be at that. You'll only go cripplin' yourself up with arthritis. Why do you keep it up? *(Puts groceries away)*

GRANDMOTHER What, in the name of God, am I supposed to do all day, Lucy, while you're to work? There's only so much knittin' and only so many rosaries to say. I do be sittin' here *(Goes to rocker)* in this chair, knittin' and saying the odd prayer, and then I sees it. You don't see it because you're too busy, but I got all the time in the world.

LUCY Sees what?

GRANDMOTHER Something grey and balled up. At

first I thinks it's a mouse gnawing his way into the corner. But when I goes over to it, it do not move. It's a wad of dust. Lucy, you don't see it, but I do on account of having nothing else to be at. So I does something about it, that's all. It's better I moves around anyway than for you to come back and see me seized up from no exercise.

LUCY Oh, Mother, just stay off your knees. They'll be swelled tomorrow and then it'll be another story about all the work you has to do around here, and I'm telling you, you don't have to do it.

GRANDMOTHER Humph!

LUCY Is Junior home? The truck is in the yard. *(Opens door and shouts out)* June!

GRANDMOTHER I heard him pull into the yard and slam the truck door to. But he never showed hisself.

LUCY No. No fear. He wouldn't. *(Becomes somewhat upset)* He's in that shed now and he won't come out till I goes in after him. And do you know why?

GRANDMOTHER When I was young we'd go into the hen-house. That was the quiet place. And the hens'ed be cluckin' away right peaceful like and it'd calm ya down if you stayed in there long enough, if you were upset like.

LUCY Mother, we don't have a hen-house. I'm askin' you if you can guess why he's in the shed and won't come out.

GRANDMOTHER He's not on the beer?

LUCY No! Junior don't drink like that and you knows it. Rubbers! Them god-blessed rubbers! I toldt him to go into Placentia and pick them out hisself, but no. "No, Mother," he says, "I don't have the time." "No time a'tall, Mother," he says, "you get 'em for me." And I said, "No, you go. Your size changes, you go in." But no sir. And I'll bet you now that he is in there with them rubbers and they don't fit him. But he's too gee-dee proud to admit it. And he'll wear them. Oh yes, he'll wear them sooner than admit they don't fit. Stubborn, just like he's father to the tee.

GRANDMOTHER I toldt you that. That Pad Joe was too stubborn to get out of his own way, but you never listened to me, did you? And stubborn begot stubborn and there you have it now, rubbers and all.

LUCY Mother, did it ever dawn on you that I married for love and that I loved Pad Joe's stubbornness? *(Takes off her shoes and sighs wistfully)*

GRANDMOTHER Ah, whist! That's all very well and grand and high spoken, but where did it ever get you, all this love business?

LUCY With a good marriage and two lovely and stubborn children. I could have done worse.

GRANDMOTHER Well, Pad Joe, the Lord have mercy on his soul, was a kind man, Lucy, of course he was. And that young fellow you got is much the same, but too stubborn for his own good he'll be, in the long run.

LUCY Did you love Dad, Mother?

GRANDMOTHER *(Startled)* Whist! What are you getting on with? All this talk.

LUCY I'm only asking if you loved him, Mother. I'm not after intimate details.

GRANDMOTHER I met him. We danced down to Sis'. He walked me along and we got married. That was that.

LUCY Signed, sealed and delivered.

GRANDMOTHER It was in the spring of the year. There was a lot to be done. You had your courtship and you posted the banns and set up house before the fall got heavy on. You don't need no big sum to figure it out.

LUCY Do you miss him, Mother?

GRANDMOTHER Miss him? Well, you'd miss the heat of a man in the bed at night. He was very thin, but there was some heat off of him for a thin man.

Lucy sighs and gives up. The door flings open and a schoolgirl enters.

GRANDMOTHER Mind. Mind right there. Wipe them! *(Points to her feet)*

MARGIE All right, Gran. Let me get this off me back, will you? I'm dead on me feet.

GRANDMOTHER Dead on your feet! Jesus Christ Almighty above on the cross! Are you after hauling up a boat? Were you laying fish? Cuttin' hay? What were you at, you poor little thing?

MARGIE Ha, ha, Gran. Very funny. Mom, is there anything to eat? I'm starved!

LUCY There's frozen french fries. There's chips and there's bars. There's a box of Kraft Dinner there somewhere.

GRANDMOTHER Chips? Bars? A box ... of food? You'd be better off eating the box for what good all that stuff will do you. Did you ever hear the like? Get yourself a slice of bread and molasses like a good Christian or stick a bit of dried fish in the stove to blacken. And stop loading down your stomach with all that junk food. Well, and they named it right, didn't they? Junk food indeed!

MARGIE Well, I'm not going so far as to eat burnt fish, Gran, but I'm stopped eating junk now. Mommy, you knows the health teacher told us to try eating raw carrots and apples and yogurt and stuff. I wants to make the basketball team this year.

LUCY Yeah, and if I puts a plateful of raw stuff onto the table, what are the chances of anyone in this house eating it?

MARGIE I dunno. I might give it a go and see if I likes it.

Lucy takes down the bars and chips from the cupboard and spreads it all out on the table.

MARGIE I might … next week. *(Reaches for a bar)* Teacher says this stuff is pure sugar.

LUCY Well, I suppose if it's pure that's something, my darling. I'd be the first one to throw this trash in the garbage, but do you think for one minute that ye crowd wouldn't be hauling it out again?

MARGIE Well, Junior wouldn't put up with it, but sure, you and me and Gran could start anyway.

GRANDMOTHER Start what?

MARGIE Eating healthy, Gran. You, me and Mom.

GRANDMOTHER Healthy? When do you see me eating junk? When? I never ate a chip in me life, or don't know what that Pepsi stuff tastes like. You're wasting your time with me. I'm miles ahead of ye. When I was growing up we were on a schedule like. You got your Sunday dinner and a cold plate in the evenings. Monday was wash day, the big wash day. That is because every day was wash day, by rights. So Mondays we'd have boiled beans. They'd be cooking on their own, see, so you wouldn't have to mind them. Then Tuesdays and

Wednesdays we'd have duck or rabbits, or what wild meat was to be had. Thursdays, salt meat again, because you'd be cravin' it, see. Friday, there'd be bang-bellies, or the fish of course, salt fish. No fat or rashers was allowed. No meat on Fridays, not like now. Nobody knows what day of the week it is when they got no religion. Funny thing Lucy … I was reading in the church paper about how we were all pagans till St. Patrick saved us, our people, I mean. And now we've come full circle … pagans again. Anyway, you know there is no bite to eat that I likes better in the week than the salt fish of a fish-Friday. Oh my, I'm a martyr to the salt fish. Saturday was cleaning day; you'd have scalded milk and scalded bread for your dinner, and a bit of fish hash for your supper. Sunday evenings you'd have the buttermilk buns too and the buttermilk cake. Everything had a schedule, not like today when …

MARGIE Mom, where is Junior? I hope he never forgot to make me those model saw-horses for my Newfoundland culture class.

LUCY He's out in the shed and he won't come in till his stomach drops out of him because he's after makin' a fool of heself.

MARGIE What do you mean? What's he at in the shed? I bet he's finishing up my models.

LUCY And sittin' down with his new rubbers on. And that's why he won't come in because his new rubbers is too small for him and he won't admit it.

MARGIE How come he got hisself a pair of rubbers too small?

LUCY He got? He never bought hisself a stitch of clothes in his life and all the other years I was sick and tired of watching him go around in rubbers too big, flopping around on his feet like great big flippers. So this time I says to him, I says, "I'm not going buying you your boots till you tells me what size." And so he says, "All right then, get me a size nine." "Nine," I says, "no way!" Well then he says, "Get me any ole size, I'll wear them." So I says to myself, I'll fix you, buddy. I'll get the nine. And you know he wastes nothing. And so he took the boots out to the shed and now he's in there and he won't come out till he's gut-founded.

MARGIE *(At the window)* There he comes now.

LUCY Don't you say nothing. Don't let on I toldt you. And ignore him if he's got them on.

The door opens and Junior comes in with a model saw-horse in one hand. All hands look at his feet. The boots are tight and crumpled around his ankles.

JUNIOR I got that done for you. It's a bit rough, but I'll plane it down after supper.

GRANDMOTHER Take them rubbers off before you comes in here. I was all day down on my knees at this floor.

Junior looks pained. Lucy breaks into laughter.

JUNIOR Mother, I thought I toldt you. A size eleven, not a ten or a nine or whatever it is.

LUCY You toldt me no such thing, Junior. You said, "Mother," you said, "get me a pair of rubbers same as last year." And I warned you to go after them yourself.

GRANDMOTHER Come in out of it and stop heatin' the harbour.

Junior hobbles in. He looks for a seat and despairingly throws himself onto the floor and tries to tug the rubbers off.

JUNIOR Margie, give us a hand. That's the girl.

MARGIE Oh my, Junior.

Margie pulls but they won't budge. Lucy goes over and holds his shoulders down.

MARGIE Are they budgin'?

JUNIOR Na, pull harder. Mom, would you leave my arms alone? You're gonna dislocate me shoulder.

GRANDMOTHER Grab aholdt to his head, Lucy, and Margie, grab his two heels, and count to three then pull.

All hands shout one, two, three.

JUNIOR Stop! Stop! Ye'll haul the legs off me. Give it up!

Junior rolls over onto his side and pulls the rubbers off with great difficulty.

LUCY So what size do you take then, June? Eight, nine, ten, or is it eleven?

MARGIE *(Picks up the model saw-horse)* That's well done, June. Sure, you could knock off a pile of them and sell them to the tourists, if you had a mind.

JUNIOR Yes, sure. That's all I got to be at now, isn't it?

Junior goes over to the television, turns it on and sits in front of it.

GRANDMOTHER There's a rabbit stew on there. It'll be ready in another hour.

MARGIE Another hour? Gran, I'm starved.

Margie goes to the fridge, takes out two frozen pizza pockets and puts them in the microwave. She sets the timer and pushes the button. There is a buzz, buzz, beep, beep. She puts the disc-man on her head.

GRANDMOTHER Stop that, for God's sake! I hates that noise. Did you ever see the like? Three stoves in the one house. One for the baby bears. One for the momma bear and one for the ole grandmother bear. *(She goes to the microwave, the electric stove and then to the old-fashioned woodstove.)* And meals going on all hours of the night and day. Just like you were runnin' a hotel. Lights on in every room whether they're in them or not.

LUCY Mother, for the love and honour of God, will you stop complaining about everything. There's nothing makes you happy. Well, I got something to tell you now that might make neither one of you happy. Will ye listen to me?

Lucy throws a cloth at Junior and waves her arms at Margie. They both look at her.

JUNIOR AND **MARGIE** *(In unison)* What?

LUCY I'm after taking in a boarder.

JUNIOR, MARGIE AND **GRANDMOTHER** *(In unison)* A what?

GRANDMOTHER Where? *(Looks around)*

LUCY You heard me … a boarder. She's not here yet. She was asking after a place up to Johnny's and Johnny toldt her about us having a spare room and all. She was in the store this evening when I stopped in there.

GRANDMOTHER A boarder? Sure, we have no need of a boarder here. With you working and Junior fishing and my bit of pension. Sure, we've no need of money. When I was rearin' ye it would have been a help all right, but nowadays we got no call for a boarder. That's Johnny Lundrigan trying to pull one over on you, Lucy, and you too blind to see it.

LUCY Pull one over on me? Why would Johnny Lundrigan want to do that? Our families have always got on. He was only trying to help the poor girl, Mother, for God's sake. I swear to God, if you had a good word to say about anyone, the heavens would open up with the fright of it.

MARGIE There's neither new teacher at the school. Is she a nurse then?

LUCY No, as a matter of fact, she works at the Cape.

JUNIOR *(Looks up from the television)* Where?

LUCY You heard me. She's from around Topsail way, Conception Bay area, I do believe.

GRANDMOTHER That's where that family of Matthews come from. I remember them livin' here when the base was being built. Every single last one of the Matthews had big teeth. They were like a crowd of beavers every Sunday in the pew, and they must have converted because Matthews is not a Catholic name. I suppose they had to on account of being out-numbered here.

JUNIOR I can't believe you're takin' in a boarder to begin with, Mother. And her working at the Cape on top of it. I'll be the laughing stock of the Shore, or worse ... I'll be accused of crossin' over.

LUCY Well, I took pity on her. She's paying a fortune up to Anthony's and she said she'd love to live in with a family.

JUNIOR Sure, she would! Mother, if you read more spy novels, you'd know that that's called "infiltration." Get among the natives and suss out what you're looking for. I can't believe you're after doing this.

LUCY Just hang on a minute! All of ye, listen to me, the three of ye! *(Throws a towel at Margie)* Ever since yer father drowned I took a backseat here. I tried to rear ye well, the way he would have wanted, the way him and me talked about rearin' ye. Now, Junior, you might be a man, but I'm still head of this family and I say it'll do no harm to welcome in a poor girl who's only trying to do her job and with no family in the area. I works all day and I hardly ever sees another soul but ye after five o'clock. I might want another person around to talk to about different things. Margie, you've always got that thing plugged into your head, and Junior, you always got your nose into a book or the television. And Mother, you're just plain too nasty to talk to. I'm sick of it! And I'll tell ye another thing that might surprise ye and that you'll have to put up with … someone is after asking me out … on a date. So I just might have a boyfriend to boot!

Look of disbelief on everyone's face. Curtains close. Lights fade.

Curtains open. Grandmother is knitting. Margie is in front of the mirror pulling down her skirt and pulling up her top. She puts on her lipstick. Grandmother is watching her.

GRANDMOTHER Where are you going with that get-up on you?

MARGIE Out!

GRANDMOTHER Oh, out. Yes, I've been there. Exciting place.

MARGIE Gran, it's Friday night! There's a dance down to the school to raise some money for the basketball team.

GRANDMOTHER You're not going playing basketball or dancing in that!

MARGIE Where's Mom to? She was supposed to give me five dollars. *(Looks at the clock)* How come she's not home?

GRANDMOTHER I don't know. Could be she's on that date, or whatever you call it, that she talked about. Or maybe she's out "getting a life," as she says. Still, it's strange for your mother not to be here after work. She's some odd these days. I never knows what she'll say, or be at.

MARGIE I'll call her and see if she's still at work. *(Goes to the phone and dials the number)* Hello, Sheila? This is Margie. Is Mom still there? All right, thanks, Sheil. Hello, Mom? Are you comin' home to supper? What? Oh … *(Pauses)* What about the five dollars for the dance down to the school? Oh, all right. *(Pauses again)* No, Gran has fish and potatoes. I'll grab a cheeseburger at the take-out. No odds. No, he's not in from the wharf yet. What? Sure, we don't know her. You're the one knows her. Oh … all right. Okay. Yeah. I'll see you before I leaves then. Okay, bye.

Margie hangs up and turns to Grandmother.

MARGIE Mom said she'll be late for supper. She said don't wait for her. She's having a drink at the hotel … with Reg. And you knows that other one from the Cape is coming over to meet us before she moves in on Sunday. Mom said she'll be back before she leaves. She said to be nice to her.

GRANDMOTHER Who, me? Why wouldn't I be? I never hurt a Christian in me life. I just hope she's not related to the Matthews, that's all. I never gave much for them, too stand-offish. No wonder they didn't last.

There's a knock on the door. Margie and Grandmother look at each other.

GRANDMOTHER Go on and answer it. Don't have her thinking we got no manners. Go on, girl.

Margie crosses over to the door and opens it. A girl is standing there in a uniform.

LILY Hello. My name is Lily Handrigan. Mrs. Connors, your mother, told me to stop by this evening to introduce myself.

Margie just stands at the door in silence.

GRANDMOTHER Margie, for God's sake, invite the girl in. Hello, come in, me child. Don't mind her, she can't talk because her lips are stuck together with all the lipstick she got smeared on them. Come in, come in.

LILY Thank you. I hope I'm not intruding, only Mrs. Connors said to come around supper time.

GRANDMOTHER No, me dear. Come on in. Lucy, that's my daughter, I'm her mother, she's still at work and said she'll be home bom by and you're to wait for her. Have you had your supper? I'm the only one to eat what I've cooked, it seems, unless Junior, my grandson, comes home. This is my granddaughter Margie here and, no, she's not having her bath. Believe it or not, she's going out dressed like that. *(Lily smiles.)*

MARGIE Gran! Mom said to say she's sorry she'll be late and for you to make yourself at home. She'll be along shortly.

GRANDMOTHER Did you have your supper yet?

LILY Well, no, I was going to go over to the take-out after …

GRANDMOTHER Take-out? Oh my. In my day you stayed in to eat and went out to go to the toilet. Now it's all reversed. Out to eat and in to …

MARGIE Gran, for God's sake! Lily. I was going to go to the take-out too, but sure, I'll stay now and we can have supper together.

LILY Oh, thanks. That'd be nice. I am kind of tired of restaurant food, to tell you the truth. It was so nice of your mother to offer me a room here.

GRANDMOTHER Yes, well, it was a bit of a surprise, to tell you the truth. We never had a boarder before. *(Grandmother goes between Margie and Lily.)* We don't know what we're supposed to do so we'll just have to treat you like one of our own. We didn't need to have a boarder, you know? We're not poor off or nothing.

MARGIE What Gran means is that we're glad to be able to help you out. That hotel must be boring this time of year with no tourists.

LILY Oh, it's okay. Just kind of lonely is all.

GRANDMOTHER Lucy tells me you're from Conception Bay. We had a family lived here in the Cove, they were from there. Matthews was their name. Ever hear tell of them?

LILY No, I can't say I have. Of course, my area has spread out a lot since I was born, with people from St. John's living there now.

GRANDMOTHER They all had big teeth ... the Matthews. You couldn't miss them.

MARGIE God, Gran, can we talk about something else? You're younger than I thought you'd be, Lily. I don't know what I was thinking, that you'd be Mom's age or something. You're working down to the Cape, right? With all the birds?

GRANDMOTHER Some smelly out there. I went with

a seniors' group a few years ago. The smell'ed cut you.
I had to keep me bandana up to my face the whole time.
My eyes were watering out of my head, it was that
strong. And to think that tourists loves it! You can't keep
a count of the trailers goes up the Cape Shore road here.
And the busloads! The tourists pays to look at the birds
from inside the building so they won't have to smell
them, see. But the government is some cute. Soon they'll
be chargin' to smell them too! Mark my words!

MARGIE Do you like working there, Lily?

LILY Oh yes, I do. I love wildlife, and the outdoors. I
love all kinds of weather too. Cold or warm, wind, rain,
snow. All of it. But I especially love watching the birds.

MARGIE You know there's something I don't
understand … something I kept meaning to ask every
time our school goes to the Cape. When they talks about
doing a bird count, how can they possibly count, and
know, how many birds are on that rock?

LILY Well …

Lucy enters and interrupts Lily.

LUCY Lily, you're here. I'm sorry I wasn't in to greet
you, but I see the family is taking care of you.

LILY *(Stands)* Oh yes, Mrs. Connors. I've been invited
for supper, although I hope I'm not imposing.

LUCY Go away, my dear! You'll have to learn how to
make yourself at home, sure, if you're going to be
lodging here. And plus you have to get a taste of the
chief cook's food to see if you likes it.

GRANDMOTHER Chief cookee and bottle-washer.
(Grandmother gets up to serve Lucy.)

LUCY And main commenter on everything. My God, Margie, you're not eatin' fish! I hope Junior braced up the roof or it'll fall in on our heads at that miracle.

MARGIE I toldt you I'm tryin' to eat healthier.
(Grandmother serves Lucy her supper.)

GRANDMOTHER You're late!

LUCY Thank you, Mother. Yes, a small bit late is all.
(Grandmother looks at the clock and makes a face.) So, Lily, do you think you'll be comfortable here?

LILY Oh yes, Mrs. Connors, I'm sure I'll be just fine.

LUCY No, right off the bat you got to stop calling me that. My name is Lucy! Margie, show Lily her room after supper, before she makes any decision about whether she's staying.

LILY Oh, I'm sure it'll be fine.

The door opens. Junior enters with a stern look on his face.

LUCY *(In a very good mood)* Junior, there you are! Come over and meet Lily, our boarder. Lily, this is my son Junior.

Lily stands up. Junior crosses the floor. Lily puts her hand out. Behind Lily, Lucy makes a fist at Junior.

JUNIOR Hello. Pleased to meet you.

Junior notices that Lily is gorgeous.

LILY Pleased to meet you too.

LUCY Lily, why don't you move yourself in here this evening? There's no reason to wait till Sunday, sure. Junior here will give you a run over and wait till you gets your bags ready. Won't you, June?

JUNIOR *(Shrugs and grunts)* Yeah.

LILY Oh … I don't know. I mean, sure. You could just drop me off, Junior. I could drive back over in my own car.

JUNIOR It's up to yourself. I'll take you over now if you wants.

LILY What about your supper? I can wait.

GRANDMOTHER Oh, Junior never eats on time anyhow. I can put it in the warmer. See, the old-fashioned gadgets is good for something.

LILY Well, all right, sure. If you're sure now it is okay.

JUNIOR Fine by me. Number one.

Everyone exits except Lily and Junior. They turn the couch on its back and he opens up the imaginary door for her. She climbs in. Junior reaches under the couch for a steering wheel. They look straight ahead for awhile. They hit a bump and both bounce.

JUNIOR Springs are bad in her. Could be bumpy.

LILY That's all right. I feel bad about you having to eat a warmed-up supper though.

JUNIOR Sure, I does that every other night. What with being at the fish and all.

LILY So you're a fisherman. Inshore or off-shore?

JUNIOR Inshore. Crab and what not. Mother tells me you works for wildlife.

LILY Well, Parks. I'm at the Cape.

JUNIOR Yeah, listen … I better tell you this right off. I hunts birds. Nothing illegal, but I just wants you to know, I'm a duck hunter.

LILY Well, there is a hunting season.

JUNIOR Yeah, and that's when I hunts.

LILY Well, here we are. Would you tell your mother I'll be over in about an hour? And thanks for the ride, Junior.

JUNIOR Yeah, sure. No problem. I'll tell Mother. No problem.

Lily exits. Junior sits there for a while thinking. He starts up the truck and puts it into gear. Says "Damn," to himself. Lights down.

Lights up. Junior swings out of the truck and slams the door. He gets off the couch, turns it around and puts the steering wheel under. The family re-enters and goes to the table.

JUNIOR She'll be over in about an hour. *(Goes to stove and gets his supper out)*

LUCY You never said anything to her, did you, Junior? Nothing saucy I hope.

JUNIOR What? Me? Sure, what would I say? That I'm a blood-thirsty son of a gun for a good feed of harlequins.

MARGIE Junior, you better be nice to her. She's sweet and she's only doing her job.

LUCY Good looking too, what, Junior?

JUNIOR I wouldn't know. She could be, I suppose.

GRANDMOTHER Where the hell is Billy Power to? He knows we starts the game at eight sharp on Friday nights.

LUCY Billy? Cards? Oh my, I forgot it's card night and Billy's coming over. Oh, and I'm after asking a friend over to meet you all.

GRANDMOTHER A friend?

MARGIE Is it the fellow who you were having a drink with at the hotel?

LUCY Yes. Reg. Reg Flynn. He said he'd stop by for a bit. *(Looks out the window)* That must be him now, or maybe it is Lily.

Knock on door. Lucy goes to door.

LUCY Reg, come in. Reg, this is my mother, Rose. My son Junior, Patrick really, but we calls him June. And this here is my daughter Margie. Everyone, this is Reggie Flynn from Placentia.

REG *(Leans out and does sideways hand-shake with Junior and lightly touches the hands of the females)* Pleased to meet you, one and all.

GRANDMOTHER Are you any relation to the funeral parlour Flynns?

REG Yes ma'am. That'd be me, along with my brothers, we own and operate the place.

GRANDMOTHER Well, it's been brought to my attention that there's after been some lot of people dying since ye opened that place!

Everyone looks at her in disbelief for a moment.

JUNIOR Gran, I don't think Reg is killin' them off himself or anything.

GRANDMOTHER No, I s'pose … I'm only saying what I sees, is all.

LUCY Reg, ah, I forgot that this is a card night, and I know we were going to go into Placentia for a game of bowling …

REG 120s? That's my game. That's fine by me, Lucy girl. A game in is as good as a game out, wha?

LUCY Yeah ... sure ... yeah ... a neighbour will come by who usually joins us.

GRANDMOTHER A neighbour? Since when did Billy Power become a neighbour? Sure, he lives half a mile up the road, almost to Branch!

LUCY Well, Mother, we're all neighbours. It's only a manner of speaking.

GRANDMOTHER Oh, that's convenient. If you pick your words right then anyone can be anything to anybody at anytime, anywhere. Neighbour the one day, boyfriend/girlfriend the next. Wakes in the home one day, stretched out a cold junk in a strange parlour the next.

REG Ma'am, what you were saying before about there being more dead people nowadays. Well, I've observed that too, since I've been in the business at least. They say though that the aging population is more. People are living longer. Then again, there's more cancer ...

GRANDMOTHER So which is it? Are they living longer or dying faster? Makes no odds as far as I'm concerned. When your time is up tis up. Sit down and we'll see if you are as good at dealing out a hand as you are at laying out a stiff. And I say the problem is not in people dying half as much as that the communities are dying. The whole Shore is an old-age home, for God's sake. Tis like another resettlement, the old being resettled to the great beyond and the young to St. John's and the mainland. God-blessed colony of ghosts here!

REG Where's your gentleman's, Lucy? Before we gets started.

LUCY Out that door at the end of the hall.

There's a knock on the door. Junior looks up from television.

LUCY That must be Billy now. *(Lucy goes to door)* Oh Lily, come on in. Junior, come help Lily with her luggage.

Junior walks towards her, but stops when she says ...

LILY Oh, it's all right. I've only one bag.

LUCY Margie, show Lily her room and get her some towels.

MARGIE All right, Mom.

LUCY Your bed is all fresh.

MARGIE Follow me, Lily.

They exit together through other side door. There's a knock on the door.

LUCY June, will you get that, luv?

Billy Power enters.

JUNIOR Billy. How are you, Billy b'y?

BILLY Junior.

Reg re-enters.

LUCY Billy! Hello. Ah, Billy, do you know Reginald Flynn from Placentia?

Reg and Billy do the sideways handshake.

BILLY Reg.

REG Billy. I think we met around town, like the saying goes.

GRANDMOTHER Come in, Billy b'y. We just put the deck on the table. We got six hands tonight. A really big shoe, as old Ed Sullivan use to say *(Does stiff Ed Sullivan movement)*

REG We got a game. *(Rubs his hands together)*

GRANDMOTHER The only game in town.

All hands draw into the table.

GRANDMOTHER I remember the last wake we had here. There was a fellow, I won't mention no names, but he was as clever as a three-headed giant. He was laying out the body and givin' this poor soul his last shave, and he spotted that the man still had his false teeth in him. "Ah, Jesus," says the man, "sure, that's a shockin' waste." So he reaches in and takes the teeth out and in order for the poor soul's jaw not to sink in, he went out to the stable and he took the shoe from off this pony and he slipped that in the fellow's mouth. An' he swore it fitted better than the teeth ever did. That he was better lookin' dead than alive.

REG Oh, there's tales from out here, that's for sure, about wakes and fellows stealin' the priest's collar and hearin' confessions. Imagine!

Lily and Margie re-enter.

LUCY Lily, this is Reginald Flynn. Reg, Lily Handrigan, our new worker out to the Cape, and our new boarder. *(They shake hands.)* And, Lily, this is Billy Power, from up the road, a neighbour.

They shake hands.

LILY Billy.

Billy nods at Lily.

REG Lily, like the flower. I see a lot of lilies in my business. Funerals. Undertaker.

GRANDMOTHER Reg here deals with the dead, but tonight he's going dealing out cards. Do you play, Lily? 120s?

LILY Well, yes, I have … a bit, not …

REG Good. You're in. That's how many now, Lucy? *(Counts heads, one, two … to five)*

LUCY And Junior for six. Lily, don't let us rope you into anything now.

LILY Oh no, Mrs. Connors … Lucy. I'd like to.

GRANDMOTHER Sure, what else is there to be at? You can't go countin' birds in the dark, right? *(Junior re-enters.)* Come on, Junnie, pull up a chair. It could be an interesting night in the ole town tonight. Billy, you're shockin' quiet tonight.

BILLY Ah, no odds. I'll pick up later, sure. Terrible heat you got here tonight, Mrs. Linehan. What are you at? Makin' anchors?

GRANDMOTHER That's my stove that's throwing all that heat, Billy. No fear the gee dee electric heat'd do that. Like throwing water on a duck's back, putting money into that plugged-in heat.

BILLY I agree with you there one hundred percent, my dear. Sure, why do you think I spends all me spare time in the woods. I'll have another load of wood for you now next week, speaking of that.

GRANDMOTHER Good man, Billy. If my husband was alive, God rest his soul, I'd have some pile of wood out by the side of the house now. But this crowd would rather give their last cent to Newfoundland Power. Not me, I thank them for the electric light, but they're robbin' us blind with the rest of it.

LUCY What are we playing? 120s? Play as we are. Mother, you deal.

REG Ah … nothing like a good game of cards, wha?

GRANDMOTHER Used to be there was nothing like a cuppa tea in the woods.

BILLY Still is. Still is nothing like a cuppa tea and a slice of bread and butter in the woods. So Reg, you're in the undertaking business? Lots of steady work there. Not seasonal like the fishery. You can always depend on people dying.

REG Oh yeah. That's for sure, Billy b'y. There do be dry spells though, long stretches, I means, when we don't see a soul, I mean a body.

GRANDMOTHER Tell me one thing, will you? Why do they call it a funeral home? Tis no more a home than it is a boiled boot. This is a home. And that room out there, that is a parlour. You know why it is a parlour? Because no one ever sits in there. But all the parlours are gone really, the ones with the lace doilies and such, the chesterfields and the paintings of Switzerland or some place.

BILLY Go on.

LUCY Twenty.

LILY Go on.

JUNIOR Pass.

REG Pass.

GRANDMOTHER Wait till I gets me glasses on. They're as thick as pond ice, but I'd be blind without 'em. Whata we got here now? Go on.

REG So Lily, you're working out to the Cape? You must spend a lot of time out of doors. Not huntin' though, wha? *(Nudges Junior and laughs)*

LILY Well, no. I don't hunt. I've nothing against it, in season and in allowed areas.

REG Oh yes, well you wouldn't catch many fellows out here doing anything illegal. Catch is the catch word. *(Winks)*

BILLY There's some do be at it, most obeys the law. Of course, we don't have much say now, do we, Junior, in when or where we can hunt, eh?

JUNIOR *(Grunts)* Huh!

LUCY Well, there had to be some restrictions or else we'd have nothing left. There's no sense in making saints where there's sinners.

JUNIOR Just would have been nice to be asked or even toldt before they slapped a closure on Briely, or Golden Bay.

LILY The reason Golden Bay is closed to hunting is because of the harlequin ducks coming back. They were almost gone from there and now their numbers are up to seven! It gives them a chance.

BILLY We was never after harlequins anyhow. Only eiders.

LILY But the hunters scared the harlequins away like.

LUCY I bid twenty.

LILY Pass.

JUNIOR Pass.

REG Pass.

GRANDMOTHER Twenty-five.

LUCY Mother, you're hot tonight.

GRANDMOTHER Hotter than love in the month of July.

All hands give her a queer look.

GRANDMOTHER Wha?

BILLY Go on. But, you know, back to the hunting thing, still, it's like we got no rights as Newfoundlanders. Our forefathers hunted for hundreds of years. Don't that give us some rights?

LILY It would if there was the same amount of birds. If some birds weren't becoming extinct. Look what happened on the Funk Islands, every last great auk taken, for feathers.

GRANDMOTHER Speakin' of extinction, wasn't there a whole crowd of Newfoundlanders extincted, if you can say that?

JUNIOR A crowd of Newfoundlanders? What are you talking about, Gran?

GRANDMOTHER Them Red Indians. The Beothuks, b'y.

JUNIOR They weren't Newfoundlanders. They were Indians, natives, or whatever like. Our crowd were the first Newfoundlanders … the Irish.

GRANDMOTHER Our crowd? Well, that's convenient. So if we had been born Indian and the Irish had killt us off, then would we, we being the Indians, have been the first settlers?

JUNIOR But we weren't, so why distort the facts?

REG What your grandmother is saying, if I may be so bold, is that it's all a question of luck, of chance. Like what we're playing. Thirty for sixty.

GRANDMOTHER Go on.

BILLY Go on, b'y.

LUCY Go on, b'y.

REG Spades.

GRANDMOTHER I was not saying that. I'm saying, if you don't protect something, like this young woman here is trying to do, there'll be nothing left.

LUCY Like the fish.

BILLY Like the fish. But it wasn't the Newfoundlanders that wiped out the cod, it was the gee dee Canadian government with giving it all away to the foreigners with trade-offs and all.

GRANDMOTHER Oh, and a Newfoundlander never over-fished, never came back from huntin' with a hundred birds on his back and then threw them away when they got the freezer burn? Like the good Lord said, "To thine own self be true."

MARGIE That was Shakespeare, Gran.

GRANDMOTHER It couldn't have been Shakespeare. I never read him.

All hands look at her in disbelief.

GRANDMOTHER Wha? Don't go givin' me them looks. I may not be educated, but I can call a spade a spade, so to speak, and by God, I believes that's what I'll call too … spades! *(Wins this hand and smacks it down on the table)* Ha, ha, not too aisy, not too aisy, at all, is the ole grandmother. Too bad we're not at it for the money, wha? I'd be haulin' in the dough tonight. How about a cuppa tea for a bit of a break? *(Gets up)*

LUCY Reg, would you like a whiskey, or a bottle of beer?

REG Oh, a nice bottle of beer'ed be grand, Lucy.

LUCY And you, Lily, cup of tea or something stronger?

LILY Oh, tea'd be grand. I'll help.

LUCY Billy? Your usual?

BILLY Yep, cuppa tea, that'd hit the spot.

LUCY June, get Reg a beer, luv, and make me a little Lambs and coke, would you?

Junior brings in drinks and then exits.

GRANDMOTHER You usually has a cup of tea and a biscuit this hour.

LUCY Yeah, well tonight I feels like something different. Why don't you take a little drink, Mother?

GRANDMOTHER Mind. *(To Reg)* Never touched the stuff in me life. No sense in pickin' up bad habits now. Waste of time, but it's not that people wastes time at all now, is it, Reg? More like time wastes them, what?

REG Oh yes, yes indeed, missus. Even in my trade you can't hold off what time does to you, only stall it a bit.

GRANDMOTHER Well time has its way. Time can fool you too, ever notice that? It lets on that it's advancin' but it's not.

MARGIE Well, time don't go backward, Gran. I'm doing a bit of physics and I knows that much.

GRANDMOTHER I'm not saying it goes backwards, or even forwards. More like it's stuck. I mean, if it went forward, then we could be able to learn, right? Say learn from the past. But if it's stuck, then you can't go forward or back and you can't learn. I has a lot of time on me hands here and I do be thinking a lot. I don't see Newfoundland advancin' any. We're still kept down by merchants, only now the merchants is the government up along, and before, they were local. That's not advancin'. And having more stuff is not advancin' *(Motions to the stoves)*, I don't think. No one knows their genealogy anymore. How's that for a word, Billy? The priest from Galway toldt me that word because I was always talking to him about where everyone is from. Now no one knows who their first cousin is, let alone their third or what part of the bay they're from. Father Fahey toldt to me where a lot of the people around here were from in Ireland. Imagine! To be able to tell that by your last name. Something wha? You knows, Lucy ... I was an O'Sullivan originally from New Ross in county Wexford, laying on the banks of the River Barrow. That kind of education is a wonderful thing.

LILY That's fascinating, Mrs Linehan! I wish I knew more about our past.

GRANDMOTHER All you got to do is ask, me child. Most information worth knowing is free. Speaking of information ... Billy, why don't you tell Lily here, and Reg, if he's interested, tell them that story about the thing that happened right after the Great Famine over in Ireland. That's a good story they never would have heard. Right up your alley there too, Reg.

BILLY I s'pose I could tell it, if you're interested. It's a story about the dead all right, kinda. Tis an old story, was toldt to me by my grandfather and he use to say his grandfather toldt him. All that crowd came over from Ireland. They were the first over. And this happened over there right after the Great Hunger, the Famine of the 1840s. After the famine there was a great plague of a sickness called choler. As if the poor people weren't hit hard enough with the famine, they then had that to try and get through. The choler spread through the country like wildfire, and a law came down that if there was a sickness on any person, you were to notice it to the Governors, or else you'd be put in jail. Well, a man's wife took sick, and he went and he did what he thought was the right thing, he went and he noticed it. They came down then with bands of men and took her away to the sick house, and he heard nothing more till he heard she was dead and was to be buried in the morning.

BILLY At that time there was such fear and hurry and dread on every person that they were burying people they had no hope of, and they with life within them. The man was uneasy thinking on that, so what did he do but slip down in the darkness of night and slip into the dead-house where they were after putting his wife. Oh, there was an awful lot of bodies about, beyond two-score, and along he went feeling from one body to the other. Then I suppose his wife heard him coming along, she wasn't dead at all. And she says, "Is that Michael?" she says. "It is then," says he, and "Oh my poor woman, have you your last gasps in you still?" "I have, Michael," says she, "and they're after setting me out here with fifty bodies the way they'll put me down into my grave at the dawn of day." "Oh my poor woman," says he, "have you the strength left in you to hold onto my back?" "Oh, Michael," says she, "I have surely." He took her up then on his back and he carried her out, and he had to carry her out past moaning bodies and those cryin' out an' saying their prayers and some grabbin' at him for help. Oh my, it was terrible. He kept on anyhow and he carried her out by lanes and tracks till he got to their house. Then he never let on a word about it, and at the end of three days she began to pick up, and in a month's time she came out and began walking about like yourself or me. And there were many people afeared to speak to her, for they thought she was after coming back from the grave. So you want to be careful, Reg, of who you're burying.

GRANDMOTHER What you want to be at, Reg, is while you're laying them out, you want to be givin' them a good whack on the head with a hammer to make sure they're dead.

MARGIE Mom, what time is it?

LUCY It's nine o'clock, honey.

MARGIE I must go down to the dance for a while.

LILY Sure, I'll give you a ride down, Margie.

LUCY It's a lovely night. I'm going to take in the air.

REG Oh, I'll join you and stretch the ole leggins' a bit.

They get up and leave. Billy doesn't look pleased. Grandmother follows them with her eyes as they exit.

GRANDMOTHER What odds about them, Billy b'y? Do you know what you'll do? Sing me a song.

BILLY Is it all right if I sings you a sad one, Mrs. Linehan? I got no heart for nothing else.

Billy sings,"The Champion of Court Hill."

GRANDMOTHER Oh my, that was wonderful. Another saucer full of tea, Billy?

BILLY Saucer full would do, ma'am. Thanks very much.

Lights fade. Lights up on Reg and Lucy walking outside. Front of stage. Reg is rubbing his hands together the whole time.

LUCY Lovely clear night. A million stars.

REG Yep. Nights like this'ed have you thinking about time like your mother was saying.

LUCY Oh, don't mind Mother. She's got to be saying something about everything. She's liable to say the opposite tomorrow, something about time moving too fast, or time draggin' like cold molasses uphill. Your best bet with Mother is to tune out.

REG Still, I likes respecting the ole folks. After all, they're the safest bet on me next dollar.

Lucy gives Reg a queer look.

REG Yeah, I got a busy couple of days now comin' up. Two brothers. Imagine, both gone the same time. Twins too. Spooky. Two ole fellows. One died twenty-four hours after the other. Natural causes. Spooky though, wha? Full dress. Full fluid injection. Yup, big day tomorrow.

Lucy looks uneasy. Lights fade.

Lights up. Junior and Lily meet outside the post office.

LILY Oh hi, Junior. Didn't expect to see you this early at the post office.

JUNIOR Yeah, tis blowy out. Didn't want to take any chances, you know?

LILY Yes, fishing must be a wonderful life. Out on the water like that, early in the morning.

JUNIOR *(Comes to life)* Yeah, yeah it is. There's great freedom in it. Yeah, I love it. *(Big smile)* I see you takes to your work too, by the mud on your boots.

LILY Yeah, well yes, I do. Crawling around on my stomach on the edge of cliffs doing a bird count. Getting trapped in fog. Seriously, though, I do. I love it because it feels so free out of doors. Kinda like your work, I s'pose.

JUNIOR S'pose. Ah, listen. There's a band down to the club on Saturday night. I mean, they're nothing special or anything, and chances are you goes to town on the weekends anyway so …

LILY No, I don't. I usually hang around my room and do up my reports. Are you telling me about the band or asking me to join you?

JUNIOR Oh, I … ah, no, join me would be all right like, if you have a mind to, I mean.

LILY What time?

JUNIOR Ah, they start around ten. Nothing formal. I mean you don't have to dress up.

LILY But I shouldn't wear my uniform. *(Grins)*

JUNIOR Well, I'd scrape the mud off your boots … I mean, be easier gettin' around the dance floor.

LILY All right. Do you dance?

JUNIOR *(Taken aback)* Oh yeah. Well, sure. I mean, don't everybody?

LILY Well, I can't waltz, okay? Just to warn you. I can't do that fancy stuff like everyone out here.

JUNIOR Nothing to that. Just follow me. I'll show you. Anyone can dance to The Arseless Men.

LILY *(Laughs)* Is that the band?

JUNIOR That's them.

LILY Okay, great. Oh, by the way, I know you're called Junior so I guess you're called after your father. So what was your father's name?

JUNIOR Oh he was Junior too. Junior Senior.

LILY Oh … kay … so … that makes you Junior Junior. *(With a grin)* See you later, Junior.

JUNIOR Yeah, right. *(Lily exits.)* Jesus, imagine that! What you do if you dares!

Junior goes back to kitchen table with a book after the post office scene and Billy knocks on door.

JUNIOR Billy.

BILLY Jun, what are ya at?

JUNIOR Not much, Billy b'y. And yourself?

BILLY Ah nothing, b'y. Nothing to be at today with that wind coming in off the Cape. Drivin' into the land something fierce, ain't it though?

JUNIOR It is. No sense contemplating it today.

BILLY No b'y. No sense in that and that's for sure. Ah, have you got a minute, Jun? There's something on me mind that I'd like to get off me chest.

JUNIOR Have a seat, Billy b'y.

Billy goes to the table and sits down.

BILLY I was just wondering, June, what you thinks of Reg, you know, with him over here the other night?

JUNIOR Oh, yeah. Reginald. Reg with the edge. Friggin' mainlander.

BILLY Well no, Junnie b'y, he's from Placentia, Reg is. Born there.

JUNIOR Same thing. Placentia might as well be the mainland. That crowd. Poisons me how they gets on.

BILLY And that's my point like. Why I came over here, like.

JUNIOR Why, Billy b'y?

BILLY What I'm saying is … Reg Flynn is after your mother, Junior b'y. He's after her, and the thing is, I don't blame him or nothing. Your mother is a fine-looking woman, if you don't mind me saying, June. I just wish she had said something to Reg about me and her.

JUNIOR You and her? You and Mother?

BILLY Yeah, I mean like the whole town knows about me and your mother.

JUNIOR Do Mother know?

BILLY Ha, ha! *(Elbows Junior)* Good one! Good one!

JUNIOR I'm serious, Billy. This could be all in your head, b'y. Mom never mentioned nothing to me, or the family. I don't think …

BILLY Well Lucy, your mother, is shy, June. She wouldn't be talking about it outright.

JUNIOR Mom's not shy, Billy b'y. I mean, I never saw you even talk to Mom any more than "good day." You talks more to me grandmother.

BILLY I was reared polite. To talk to the old people. And I don't need to talk to your mother, June.

JUNIOR Oh, Billy, I think you do. Mom's a talker. Mom do like to discuss things … a lot.

BILLY *(Put out)* Well, I've known your mother since we were children, June, so I think I got a bit more background on her.

JUNIOR Yeah, well, how come she never married you then? She married my father, in case you didn't notice.

BILLY Yeah, I noticed. That was when I went up to Lab City that spring. I don't hold that against her though, June.

JUNIOR Jesus, Billy b'y, you're worse off than I thought. Maybe Mom'd be better off with Reg what got the edge. Big show that he is. Anyway, she's not interested in either one of ye arseholes. Mom's got more going for her than either one of ye.

Billy sits looking despondent. Junior just stares straight ahead. Lights down on Billy and he exits.

Lights up on Junior. Junior is sitting on couch reading. Lucy comes out of the back room carrying a box. Her hair is tied back with a scarf.

JUNIOR Mom, it's Saturday. Why don't you do something else besides work. That back room can wait.

LUCY Wait? Wait for what? I want to get it cleared out while I got a minute.

JUNIOR Now you sound like Grandmother.

LUCY Oh Jesus. God forbid. My worse nightmare, that I turnt into your grandmother. Doing everything just so she can complain about it afterwards.

JUNIOR C'mon, Mom, let's go to Gooseberry. Look at that sun! How often do we get sun like that and a Saturday together at the one time?

LUCY Gooseberry? What do I want at Gooseberry beach at my age? It's different when ye were small. All the mothers'd take the youngsters then. What would I want to go there now for and you grown up?

JUNIOR We'll sun ourselves. Bring your bikini. C'mon, I'm not taking no for an answer. Just me and you. We'll go for a dip.

LUCY All right then. Let's pack a lunch and grab a few towels to stretch out on. It'd be nice to hear the ocean and see the sun dancin' off the water now, wouldn't it? But I don't swim, June, and you knows that so ...

JUNIOR Mom, we can't go to the beach without gettin' in the water. On a day like today ...

LUCY No way, Junior! Let's get that straight right now before we head out. I'm steering clear of the water, so leave me in peace there. You're the water dog.

JUNIOR How come you never learnt how to swim anyway, Mom?

LUCY Because your grandmother wouldn't let me. Afraid if I learnt how to swim, I might drown.

JUNIOR *(Nods for a while)* Yeah, that sounds like Grandmother all right. I'll just grab me swimming trunks.

LUCY And I'll make us a few ham sandwiches and a thermos of tea.

JUNIOR *(Calls out while walking off stage)* Let's get there before the sun runs off!

At the beach.

JUNIOR How was your night last night, Mom?

LUCY Oh, all right, Junior honey. You know.

JUNIOR No, I don't know. I never went out with Reg myself.

LUCY *(Laughs)* Hard to get a word in with him, I must say that. He sure loves to hear hisself talk. But at least I got out of the house. Next weekend we're going to town for the day.

JUNIOR St. John's? What are you going at in there?

LUCY Some casket showcase thing or other. And we'll have lunch somewhere, which is the nice part.

JUNIOR Funny, you going off places now. It's good, I mean. Good you're getting out and stuff.

LUCY Yeah, yeah it is, Junior. I mean Reg is nothing serious like, but he's an all right companion, in his own way.

JUNIOR Likes a game of cards.

LUCY Likes a game of cards.

JUNIOR He's outgoing and talks. The opposite of Billy Power. That's good.

LUCY Yeah, sure is the opposite of Billy. Billy's idea of a conversation is a few shrugs and saying "Good day."

JUNIOR And then thinks he's courtin' you.

LUCY Then thinks he's got it knocked. Sewn up.

JUNIOR In the bag. Done for. At the altar.

LUCY Game over before it began. *(Pause)* Is Lily to work?

JUNIOR I s'pose. Not much else for her to be at in these parts, is there? *(Pause)*

LUCY She's nice, Lily, isn't she, Junior?

JUNIOR Oh yeah. Lovely. I mean nice, yeah, and lovely too, yeah, I s'pose.

LUCY I saw you talkin' to her outside the post office yesterday. Anything special?

JUNIOR Nah. Same ole flyers and the odd bill.

LUCY *(Elbows him)* She's a nice girl, Junior. Sweet, and smart too.

JUNIOR Oh yeah, and educated and on the move and super independent.

LUCY So what? Don't put yourself down just because she's aiming high or put her down for it because of her job.

JUNIOR Jeez, Mom, I'm not. She puts all her cards on the table. I know where she stands with her job and I even respects her for it. Anyway, there's no sense talking about something when nothing is goin' on. Not to change the topic or anything, Mom, but I was talking to Billy the other day.

LUCY Billy? Billy Power? Yeah, and ...

JUNIOR Well ... did you know Billy expected you to wait for him when he got back from Lab City?

LUCY What?

JUNIOR Twenty-five years ago.

LUCY What in God's name are you talking about?

JUNIOR Ah, never mind. You're not interested in Billy Power, are you, by any chance?

LUCY Oh, God save us and preserve us. Junior b'y, the ole cat Trixie that's been dead for seven years got more life than poor ole Billy.

JUNIOR Well, what do you think he do be doing coming over here for cards every Friday night?

LUCY So what! What do I owe Billy Power? Nothing. That man knows nothing about women or courtship or nothing else, except the woods, I'd say. Not that he's a bad sort.

JUNIOR Well, Billy thinks yer courtin'. There's an awful lot going on in Billy's head that you don't know about.

LUCY It can stay there. It's not my job to go rootin' information out of his head, or any man's. I'm not going to be interested in someone because they're interested in me. I owes him nothing.

JUNIOR Mom, you loved Dad a lot, didn't you?

LUCY Loved him? Now there was a man with no fear in him and that was the life of him and the death of him, God rest him. He was everything. There was nothing missing in your father, Junior. Not a god-blessed thing.

JUNIOR Did you know that loons mate for life, Mom?

LUCY I'm not a loon, June. I'm not even your mother anymore. You don't need a mother anymore. June, sometimes I get the feeling that you think I won't walk in that door one evening. But, June, because your father is gone don't mean I'll disappear. You got to let go of that. Let go of me. *(Pause)* Now let's get home out of it before I'm red as a lobster and too burnt up to dance tonight.

JUNIOR You're going to the dance tonight too?

LUCY I certainly am. One thing I'll say for Reg ... he's a good sport.

JUNIOR Oh, Reg is going too?

LUCY I'm hardly going alone.

JUNIOR And Billy?

LUCY The only one missing will be your grandmother!

JUNIOR I'll ask her if you wants. Have all hands on deck. *(Lucy smacks at him.)* I'll bet Gran dances like Ed Sullivan. *(Does Ed Sullivan imitation. Lucy joins in and they waltz off together in Ed Sullivan imitation.)*

Lights up on Lucy's kitchen. Lucy and Billy sitting at table.

BILLY I dunno. I always thought maybe nothing had to be said. You know, Lucy?

LUCY No, Billy, I don't know. I really don't know. I don't know how nothing had to be said. I really don't.

BILLY Oh.

LUCY You got to say something, Billy.

BILLY I was coming over. Every Friday night I was over and you were here and we played cards. And then Reg showed up.

LUCY Wait! Back up there, Billy. Every Friday night you were coming over and we played cards. Did you think that was asking me out? You coming here?

BILLY Well, yeah. I was coming here to see you … and well, to play cards and all.

LUCY But not to ask me out.

BILLY There's nowhere out to go to, Lucy. Where could we have got to?

LUCY But, Billy, was this supposed to go on forever? You coming here every Friday night till one us died off?

BILLY No, I would have asked you to marry me sooner or later, Lucy.

LUCY Marry you! And what if we'd a had nothing in common or nothing to say to each other?

BILLY What do you have in common with that Reg Flynn? And he talks at you not to you.

LUCY I know all that, but he asks me out. He shows an interest.

BILLY I was always interested in you, Lucy. Way back, before Pad Joe, God rest him.

LUCY Well, Pad Joe didn't know no more than I did about anything. Jesus, Billy b'y, you can't just expect people to know what's in your head.

BILLY Yeah … so, you're not interested? Like that, I mean.

LUCY No, Billy. Not like that.

BILLY And Reg? I mean it's none of my business …

LUCY Well, you can inquire anyway. But I'm not telling you.

Margie and Lily are sitting at kitchen table.

MARGIE Lily, your hair is gorgeous. All those braids. That must have took a keen spell to do?

LILY Yes, girl. Eight hours.

MARGIE And it must have been a keen price?

LILY Yeah, cost me an arm and a leg.

MARGIE Did you always want to be a biologist, Lily, and work at wildlife?

LILY Yeah, I knew I had to get outdoors and work. I'd go nuts if I had to stay in an office all day. What about you, Margie, what do you want out of life?

MARGIE Oh well. Can I tell you my wildest dream and

then I'll tell you what I'll probably settle for? I'd love to be an actress! Imagine! Don't tell anyone … promise! This place is a carousel of eyeballs watching.

LILY   I won't. So … what will you probably settle for?

MARGIE   Oh, I'll probably teach or something so I can maybe live out here.

LILY   Do you act in plays in school?

MARGIE   Do I ever! Wouldn't miss a one. Gran tells me I'm the biggest mocker on the Shore. She says I can do anyone.

LILY   Do Gran.

MARGIE   Do Gran?

LILY   Yes, go on.

MARGIE   Okay. Here she is … *(Margie does: "Mind, mind right there. Wipe 'em." "Ah whist, Lucy." "You any relation to them Matthews? They all had big teeth." "Really big show tonight, b'ys." "Not too aiesy is the old grandmother. Not too aiesy.")*

Grandmother enters.

MARGIE   Gran! You're back already? I mean where were you to?

GRANDMOTHER   Over to the church, cleaning it up like I does every Saturday. What are ye girls doing in on such a fine day? Afraid of the fairies takin' ya?

LILY   Do you believe in fairies, Mrs. Linehan?

GRANDMOTHER   Believe? What's not to believe? You can't see them, so how can you believe in 'em? But they does enough mischief not to believe in them. So whichever way you want. Put the kettle on, Margie, that's the girl. I'm parched for a cuppa tea and a biscuit.

LILY Do you believe in witches? I'm curious about all that stuff.

GRANDMOTHER Same thing. What's not to believe? My uncle had the witchery in him and he had to put it to use one time with a changeling. There was a woman here wouldn't talk. She was gettin' on in age and this fellow, Jimmy Heaney, wanted to marry her. They knew each other since youngsters, and then she, Alice O'Keefe she was, God rest her soul, then she was all spirit and good looks. But one day she changed, just like that. She became withdrawn into herself and she stopped talking. Well, everyone left her alone, like they use to them times. No head doctors, no pills back then, like there is now. Pill for everything, did you ever notice that? And any little worry at all, it's off to have a great long discussion about it. Anyway, she was left alone and one day Jimmy gets it into his head to marry her, and oh my God, you'd think he was asking for her hand to lead her into war. So Jimmy came to my uncle and said it was a queer thing Alice never wanted to get married and her good-looking one time and now with a good bit of land and a cozy house in the bargain. And Jimmy wondered if my uncle could "see" whether or not she might be a changeling.

GRANDMOTHER My uncle said that there was a rumour about her, on account of a dog barking all night one night when she was there alone and then the dog never barking again after that. Well, me uncle said there's one way to find out. Go to her and ask that person standing there if she's Alice and hold up the holy picture in front of her. And he did and he said he kept talking at her saying, "What did ye do with our Alice? Where did ye put her? Bring her back this minute." He commanded her to not rise up in the air and fly over the way. Oh, he went on and on in that manner, and her all the time frightened to death. He rapping the ground with his big stick and yelling out, "I'll open up the ground and get the devil up from hell to take you." And he swore the ground started trembling and him yelling the devils were coming and for the freak, the changeling, to banish and bring back Alice. And didn't she grab hold to the picture and squeeze it against her chest and then he knew he had Alice. But there was no change in her though. That's the way he toldt it to me. My, that's some grand cuppa tea. *(Grandmother moves in the same way as girls were making fun of earlier.) Lights fade.*

Lights up on bar scene. Billy is standing at the bar at the dance. All hands enter.

JUNIOR Billy. How are you tonight, Billy b'y?

BILLY All right, s'pose.

JUNIOR Grand day today, Billy.

BILLY Yup, grand.

JUNIOR Why don't you come over to the table and join us? Plenty of room.

BILLY *(Looks over at the table)* Nah, think I'll keep the bar up here. Five's a crowd.

JUNIOR Up to yourself. I never saw you dance. Do you dance, Billy?

BILLY You asking?

JUNIOR Ha, ha. Dancin's a way to get the women, b'y. Women loves to dance.

BILLY Yeah? I'll keep that in mind.

JUNIOR Beer, Billy?

BILLY *(Shows his beer)* No thanks.

JUNIOR Righto. Catch you later. *(Junior walks back to table with drinks.)*

REG C'mon, Lucy. Let's break the ice for the crowd. We'll be the first up.

LUCY Oh all right. Might as well jump right in.

JUNIOR Mind. You can't swim.

LUCY Use to be a wicked dancer though.

JUNIOR C'mon, Lily. Let's you and me give her a go.

LILY Sure.

All hands dance to Merle Haggard's "Wake Up" and when the song ends, they sit back down at the table. Reg goes up to the bar.

REG Billy. Beer, Billy?

Billy holds his beer high in the air to indicate he has one.

REG Right. So ... how are you?

BILLY Lovely. Grand. Super.

REG Haul your chair over to the table, Billy b'y, and join us.

Billy looks behind him for "his chair," sarcastically.

BILLY Me chair?

REG Or whatever. Up to yourself.

Reg gets drinks. Walks back to the table. Sits down and begins talking as if he never left.

REG So I says, Jeez, b'y, I dunno, didn't ya see the sign? NO FAGS ALLOWED! *(Reg roars laughing.)* Fags right? Tyin' in with the no smoking in bars now, but not meaning the cigarette like. *(No one laughs.)* I laughed meself sick when I heard that one. Thought it was right sharp.

Reg laughs a lot, rather uncomfortably, because no one else joins him. Lights fade. All hands exit the bar scene.

Lights up. Lucy, Junior and Lily enter from the main door. All are a little tipsy.

LUCY Shush. Shush. Or whist. Whist. As your grand-mother would say.

JUNIOR She'll be down aboard of us if she hears she's talked about. You know she's got hear-through ears on her.

LILY Would anyone like a cuppa tea, or is it too late?

LUCY Never too late for a cuppa tea, my dear. Yes, make us one, Lily. *(She takes her shoes off and rubs her feet.)* Oh my, I forgets what it's like to dance. Pure murder if you're not use to it.

JUNIOR *(Comes over to the couch and sits down)* I'm after scarin' Reg off, ain't I, Mother? When you and Lily went to the bathroom I toldt him I didn't think you'd appreciate the kind of jokes he toldt.

LUCY I hope you toldt him you didn't appreciate them either? I never reared ye to be ignorant.

JUNIOR Yes, Mom, you know I did. And, Lily, I included you too, just in case like … I hope you don't mind.

LILY Mind? Did you see me laugh? Sure, your mother and I both said it wasn't the least bit funny.

LUCY Sometimes a few drinks loosens the tongue a bit too much, wha? Better to find out now. He did apologize when we were saying goodnight, except he really didn't seem to know what he was sorry for. It all seemed like we were making a big deal out of a "little joke" to him.

LILY It was like that for me when I was going to university. Everywhere you turned there was a so-called harmless joke about someone, gays, blacks, Jews, Pakistanis, Newfoundlanders.

JUNIOR I can't stand Newfie jokes.

LILY Lots of Newfoundlanders are the worst perpetrators of Newfie jokes, Junior. It's like we don't mind being made fun of, or feeling bad about ourselves. Like it's a birthright or something ... and so we call ourselves Newfies and let others call us that too.

JUNIOR It's mostly Newfoundlanders livin' away does that.

LILY No, it's not. It's all over the island too. And another thing I hates is the gee dee Screech-Ins. Gettin' tourists to kiss a dead codfish or a plastic one. Imagine! I don't know which is worse, the real dead one or the plastic one. Says lots about who we are, doesn't it?

LUCY As if the codfish was a symbol of who we are anymore. People marching out of rural areas, that's more a symbol, that's for sure.

LILY Why can't we just be ourselves, the best of ourselves for the tourists and for ourselves? I sees all kinds out at the Cape and most goes out there are sensible people, they're embarrassed at the notion of kissin' a fish or hearin' a Newfie joke. I'm not ashamed of being a serious person.

LUCY Who knows how to have a bit of fun.

LILY Yes, sure.

JUNIOR And knows how to old-fashioned waltz when she said she didn't!

LILY Sure, who wouldn't know how to waltz with you guidin'?

Lucy lifts her eyebrows in approval.

JUNIOR So, Mom, you talked to Billy and now you come home alone tonight. Three strikes and you're out!

LUCY Out? Out of wha? The dating game? Oh my, it does seem like a lot of work when you hits my age. I'd like to keep Billy as a friend, a family friend like he always has been. And Reg, well, I'm not going to hold his biases against him when he apologized. He's a friend too. And having a friend is nothing to scoff at … Junior … what's that phrase you use when you're duck hunting, the one about where your hunting dog goes into the water after a duck, but the duck is not dead, it's only wounded?

JUNIOR Chasin' cripple. The dog goes after the duck and the duck is able to swim away fast, but not fly away 'cause its wing is wounded. And so the dog exhausts itself goin' after it.

LUCY And drowns from exhaustion.

Grandmother appears in her bathrobe, rubbing her eyes and yawning.

GRANDMOTHER No fear of any of ye drowning from exhaustion.

LUCY Mother! What are you doing up? Did we wake you?

GRANDMOTHER Lucy, you may be a full-grown woman, but I still can't sleep till ye are all home in bed. And I expect I'm not the only mother was ever like it. S'pose I'll have a mug up with ye. *(Gets a cup of tea)*

LUCY Mother, how would you feel about up and leaving the shore? Or Newfoundland for that matter?

GRANDMOTHER What? To do what? What are you talking about now, Lucy girl? I can't keep up with you.

JUNIOR What are you saying, Mother? Leave?

LUCY I'm only inquiring as to how any of ye feels about it. I've been thinking about that phrase of yours "chasin' cripple." I mean rural Newfoundland to me is like a lame duck and we're the exhausted dog swimming further and further out to sea.

GRANDMOTHER You into the Lambs? Listen, my child, I know what you're saying. There's not much whisper of a future for the younger crowd, is there? You're thinking of Junior here and Margie, I know.

LUCY Actually, I was thinking of meself. I might want to get away. Junior is reared and Margie is nearly. Then what'll I be left with?

GRANDMOTHER Me.

JUNIOR Sure, Mom, what about your job hair-dressing? You've worked at Sheila's for over ten years.

LUCY Exactly. A hairdresser can get work anywhere in a city or town. I'm only saying, Junior. I'm looking at me options. I mean, look at the Shore, it's a ghost town. There's no one. Everyone I went to school with is gone. Junior, almost everyone your age is gone. Margie'll be gone.

GRANDMOTHER And I soon enough. I'll be gone to the home or into Reg's hands. Jesus, Mary and Joseph. I never thought I'd see the place go from the poverty of the old times to the poverty of spirit on the go now. Working for E. I.? Is that any way to live? My father, God rest him, toldt me work is everything and he was right. There's an awful crushin' to the spirit going on.

LILY But what can people do, most of the work is seasonal?

GRANDMOTHER That's right. But the people aren't seasonal anymore. Where do your carrots come from? Read the bag … California or Ontario! God save us. Nobody got a garden. Everybody got a lawn though.

LUCY But, Mother, times change. That's the nature of time.

GRANDMOTHER Fair enough. But does change have to cause ignorance. The young crowd knows more about that … Brad Pitts than they do about their grandfathers 'cause that's what they're interested in. They never met Mr. Pitts or Mr. Snoop Dog. What about Patsy Judge and Mickey McGrath. The knowledge in them men, who got it now?

All hands are silent.

GRANDMOTHER Chasin' cripple. I'll be chasin' meself soon enough. That's it, *(cup empty)* last drop drained. Don't stay up trying to change the world now. There's people paid for that and they can't get it right, not in one night anyhow.

LUCY Goodnight, Mother.

GRANDMOTHER Mass at nine o'clock. I don't be pressin' the altar cloths for the Lord alone.

LILY I'll follow you, Mrs. Linehan.

JUNIOR Goodnight.

LUCY Goodnight.

Grandmother and Lily exit.

JUNIOR *(Rinses his cup)* Mother, don't trouble yourself no more tonight. Rome wasn't built in a day. Get a good rest now. *(Kisses her on the top of the head)*

LUCY Junior hon', would you wake up Margie?

JUNIOR *(Shakes Margie roughly and playfully.)* Margie, Margie, wake up, Margie.

LUCY Good night, Margie. Goodnight, June. See you in church, as they say. *(She sits alone on the chair in silence.)* Rome wasn't built in a day. So should I stay in Rome and do as the Romanians do? Pad Joe, what should I do? All I got is questions and no answers, Pad. *(Silence)* Junior will stay here as long as there's fish to be caught, and how long is that? He loves the water the same as you, Pad. And he'll have hisself a wife when the time is right. And Margie'll go. That leaves me with Mother. Hmmm ... and this lonely, lovely stretch of Cape Shore. *(She goes to stage right and unhooks the curtain, then to stage left and unhooks the other curtain.)* It's almost as lonely now as when the first settlers came. I'd say Mother was right ... all the gadgets got everyone kept in out of doors. It's hard to know what to be at. *(Catches curtain and draws curtains toward centre)* Hard to know. *(Closes curtain completely)*

A FAMILY OF STRANGERS

Approximately 50 minutes

A Family of Strangers was produced in 2006 at the Cuslett Community Arts Centre.

A grandmother, mother and daughter are at the centre of this play. Three generations moving in and out of each other's lives. When illness strikes the older woman, all rally around her. Dark family secrets creep out. The play also deals with the idea of a different type of family unit when the youngest of the three decides to help her girlfriend raise a child.

LIST OF CHARACTERS & ACTORS (2006 PRODUCTION)

GRAN: Mildred Dohey
MARGIE: Nicole Conway
LUCY: Kay Coffey

Lights up. An old woman is sitting by the window in her kitchen. Sometimes she is still and sometimes she is rocking. She is staring and staring and then lets out a sigh.

WOMAN No chance of a sunny break. No chance of a break at all. Unless I falls. Good chance I'd break me hip then. Only break I'd get, I'd say. Oh my. *(Picks up her knitting, rocks back and forth and hums to herself)* Funny ole life. Queer ole life. One time I couldn't get a single solitary second to meself. House full all the time. Sunrise to sunset, always on the tramp. From diaper to dustpan. From baking bread to laying fish. From laying fish to peeling potatoes. Peeling potatoes to helping with the homework. You'd have to go to the toilet to get a minute alone. Pretend you had a bad cramp or something. Bring in the *Reader's Digest* in order to get a chance to read it. In order to get a chance to mind something different. Youngsters always bawling and fighting. Always hungry. Always tormenting each other. Always dirty and snot-nosed. And now … you'd swear I never had one. You'd swear I was an old maid. The phone rings twice a year, Christmas and me birthday. Sometimes only once a year. Soon not even that, I suppose. I remember old Mrs. Lundrigan said, she said, "You're supposed to raise your children to be independent … like the birds does. Drive them from the nest. Give 'em a push off the cliff. Well, oft the doorstep, I s'pose, for youngsters. Let them make their way in the world." Humph! Maybe I give 'em too hard a push! *(Folds her knitting away)*

WOMAN Well, no sense sitting here feeling sorry for meself. That won't get me very far. Not that there's far to go, now, mind you. These legs wouldn't get me far now anyhow. *(She looks down at them, sizes them up, pulls up her dress a bit and makes a face.)* There was a time when me doing that would drive the young fellows nuts. Not that I did it now, mind you. But you didn't have to in order to know the sway you had over the young fellows.

I was a keen good-looker. Yes, I was. In my day, yes sir. At the dances in the night down to the hall, the boys would be lined up on one side and the girls on the other, and I never had a problem gettin' a dance. More of a problem keeping 'em off me. Oh well, and now me legs, sure, you can't tell the bottoms from the top. And what slim ankles I had one time. Delicate, like the neck of a swan. Oh yes. And now, it's like they belongs to someone else. I don't recognize meself in them. It's like I woke up one morning and someone had screwed the wrong legs on me. I think I got old Mrs. Lundrigan's legs by mistake. She always had legs like a bull terrier. Walked like a Sumo wrestler. God rest her, the poor soul. The foulest breath on a creature ever breathed too. Like she ate boiled cabbage every meal of her life. Well, she'll not be breathing on anyone now.

The phone rings.

WOMAN What's that? Who'd be calling me? Hello? What? Oh, all right, girl, I s'pose. Who? When was that? Oh, yes. Yeah. Yeah. Wha? You don't know. You don't know, my dear. How old was he? Sure, you knows what kilt him. Yes. Make no mistake. Liquid diet they calls it. Yeah. Chain-smoked? Kept the cigarette companies in business, my dear. You watch now the big crash on Wall Street. Wall Street. The stock market. Oh, never mind. How's Lottie? What operation? They took what out? What? Never knew we had one of them. Down around where? I don't have one. No odds. Elsie who? Oh yes. She got what? Sure, there's needles for that, girl. That's extinct for years, that disease. No, that's true. There's diseases now were never around before. What? Sure, that's bad nerves, what we'd call low-minded. Called what? Sure, having something called that'd drive you nuts. She do be what? Sure, that's nerves. Well, no I don't, but other people do. She don't need no pills for that. Do her confession with the priest is all. Bernard should be taking them pills and not her. What? All right. Yes I'm going. You going? All right, all right then, girl. All right. *(Tries to put the receiver down, bends her head into the phone to get the person to hang up)* All right then, girl. Yeah. All right, all right. Yeah. *(Hangs up and sighs)* Poor soul. She got no one to talk to. *(Sighs, folds her hands in her lap, gets up, goes to the window, sits down, draws back the curtain and looks out)*

WOMAN Not much activity. No one on the go. Except them that's leaving. Alice's husband went up to Alberta a couple of months ago. She swore she'd never go … No way, she said. And now Alice is gone. Packed her bags up two weeks ago, and her two teenage daughters went with her. For the summer, she said. Only for the summer. But the whole works of them got jobs right away. And I mean right away. Hardly had the fog wiped off their glasses and they were punching the clock. Good money too, she said. So what do they have to come back to? Maybe the girls to finish school, but after the summer, they'll be set up there and then they'll head back up. Can't blame them. My God, no. What's here? A fish plant on crutches. And I don't mean stilts like the wharves and sheds all use to be years ago. That was lovely, growing up, to go out on the wharf or to your father's shed on the water in the morning and hang your bare legs over the wharf. The seagulls would be screeching and the waves rolling and rolling. So peaceful. I loves any building built over the water. I saw on the television one time, somewhere in the South Seas, the way people live. Tiny houses up on stilts in the water and nice warm breezes all the time. And the hotels next to them. I'd live in a house on stilts any time over a hotel with a maid.

WOMAN Where was I? The fish plant on crutches is where I was to. A wing and a prayer. Is that any way to live? One thing I don't understand. Way back in the hard times, when no one had a cent, when we had only the one dress, we looks back on that and calls it the depression or hard times. We owned our own homes ... paid for. We had a boat ... paid for. We ate good healthy food and everyone was there to help everyone else. Now there's money galore and credit cards and everyone is paying a mortgage, car payments, boat payments, cable and satellite, and the internet thing, phone and lights and groceries by the car full. No one can live here. No work. And I heard on the television the other day how we lives in what they call the global village. The world is that small. If it's so small, how come no one ever comes to visit? And if there's so much money around, how come everyone got to go away? Is Danny Williams that much of a townie? And family? Sure, that's almost a dirty word now. It's like you're cursed if you has family. They're there, but they're not there. Family of strangers now is what we all are. Oh my.

There's a knock on the door.

GRANDMOTHER Who can that be? Who'd be visiting me? Hello? Come in, I s'pose.

MARGIE Hello, Nan.

GRANDMOTHER Who's that?

MARGIE Oh Nan, you know who I am. It's Margie, your granddaughter.

GRANDMOTHER Margie? Granddaughter? I don't have a granddaughter.

MARGIE Now stop that now, Nan. You knows you do.

GRANDMOTHER I use to have a granddaughter. And a daughter. But I think they must have disappeared off the face of the Earth or got amnesia. That's an illness you never hear tell of anymore, so it can't be that.

MARGIE Nan, you know Mom went to Fort MacMurray. She calls you.

GRANDMOTHER Oh yes. That's right. Lucy, is it her name? Lucy, did she have red hair?

MARGIE Nan, that's not fair. Mom's working all the time. It's not like when she was home here.

GRANDMOTHER Working all the time? Yes, I suppose she got to support her habit.

MARGIE *(Shocked)* What habit? Mom don't got no habit.

GRANDMOTHER "Don't *have* no habit."

MARGIE What?

GRANDMOTHER The proper English is, "Don't have no habit." Not "don't got." Not that I knows a lot about education, but I knows that. What are they teaching you at the university, if you don't know that much?

MARGIE They're teaching me education. I'm going for my education degree.

GRANDMOTHER Education degree? And you don't know not to say "don't got"?

MARGIE I s'pose I don't. I don't talk like that in St. John's anyhow. But I didn't come to visit you to talk about the bad education I'm getting, Gran. How are you?

GRANDMOTHER You don't talk like that in town? Oh, only around us crowd, is it? That's precious. How am I? Another year older and no deeper in debt. Thank God. And speaking of debt, you must be up to your eyeballs in it now, I expect, paying for that what you calls an education.

MARGIE Sure, what else am I s'pose to do, Gran? There's nobody going to give it to me free, now, is there? And what else am I supposed to do with me life?

GRANDMOTHER You could come back here and take care of your grandmother.

MARGIE That's not fair, Gran. And you knows it. So if I did that, then what am I supposed to do after you're gone? And then I'd have no education, no job, no money, no nothing.

GRANDMOTHER You'd have this house. You'd have the peace of mind knowing that someone took care of me in my old age.

MARGIE That's just not fair for you to say, Gran.

GRANDMOTHER And what's wrong with staying around here? All your people did it before you. That's how come you were born here. Did you ever think of that? And you could settle down with some fellow from here.

MARGIE Oh, yeah, right. Like who? Any prospects?

GRANDMOTHER I don't know who do be on the go nowadays. If ole Bessie McGrath was alive, she'd know who was on the go. She was the matchmaker for this place. She knew just who to match up with who.

MARGIE "With whom."

GRANDMOTHER Wha?

MARGIE "With whom." It's supposed to be "with whom."

GRANDMOTHER We never talked like that around here. That was the English crowd that said the "whoms" and the "thous." We were never grand out here.

MARGIE So did she match up many, or wha?

GRANDMOTHER Many? Almost everyone. Except them that were beyond matching. If you knows what I means.

MARGIE No, I don't. But we won't go there.

GRANDMOTHER Of course everyone she matched took. She knew her job. She had a way with that sort of thing. Like midwives would, or water diviners. She had a feel for it and she never lost a case, as the lawyers say. Everyone stayed happy together.

MARGIE Well, who knows about that. I'd say the church had a lot to do with people staying together, and the economics. I don't say love had much to do with it in all the cases.

GRANDMOTHER Love. Love. Where did love ever get anyone? For God's sake, my dear. Love is after doing more harm now than warfare. All they talks about on the television and on them silly songs on the radio is love, love, love. Love is all you need. Love is what makes people live together instead of under the holy sacrament of marriage. And do them people stay together, do they? No, they do not. But if they took it seriously and got married at the very beginning of going around together, then it would last. I'm telling you.

MARGIE Gran, sometimes your logic is so convoluted that even I think you could be right.

GRANDMOTHER Yes, you're damn right I am! So, you never toldt me ... what brings you out here? Now?

MARGIE I had some time away from the books and the part-time job. I thought I'd get away and see you for the weekend.

GRANDMOTHER For the weekend? Oh my. You

mean to say you're not just dartin' in and dartin' out? That'd be a first.

MARGIE Gran, I'm not going getting into an argument with you. Every time I comes out you acts like you wants to drive me away.

GRANDMOTHER I do not. You're always on the tear is the thing. Always making arrangements on the cellar phone or on that flat top or lap top or whatever it is you calls it. Here's something I don't understand … the crowd going now have got all kinds of ways to stay in touch with one another. Ye knows each other's every move. But do ye actually ever see one another? Ye talks to one another on the phone, and ye clicks away to one another on that computer thing. But do ye ever sit down and have a cup of tea with one another and ask the other how it's going?

MARGIE Times have changed, Gran. No one drinks tea anymore. It's more like coffee shops or we has a beer.

GRANDMOTHER Ye has a beer. Glory be to God. In my time, only the men drank, at Christmas or the odd special time, a garden party dance or something. What could be had from St. Peter's down off Fortune. Do you be drinking?

MARGIE Well, yeah, sometimes like.

GRANDMOTHER Sometimes like what? You're not the legal age for that. You're only barely eighteen.

MARGIE Well, Gran, nobody waits to be legal … God. There's ways of getting beer, you know.

GRANDMOTHER Yeah, and there's ways of gettin' in trouble and the beer is the real way. What do you want to be guzzlin' that ole dirt for? Bringing trouble on yourself. Why do you need that?

MARGIE I don't need it, Gran. It's just a social beer and I don't be guzzling it ... God.

GRANDMOTHER God, God, God. Well speaking of Himself. It's Saturday night and time for Sunday mass. I suppose you lost your religion when you took up the beer, did you? Or when you moved to St. John's?

Grandmother puts on her coat and bandana. She picks up her rosary beads.

GRANDMOTHER Mind, you don't let that fire go down now. I'll want a cuppa tea when I gets back. And maybe something that you bake ... that blueberry crumble thing with the porridge that you made the last time was tasty enough.

MARGIE That was with raw oats and brown sugar, Gran ... but whatever ... I'll make something. I brought out some stuff, some ingredients like.

GRANDMOTHER Wouldn't hurt you to run through the rosary while I was gone, even though you're so anti-church.

MARGIE Yeah, Gran, sure ... whatever.

Grandmother exits mumbling.

GRANDMOTHER Yeah ... sure. *(Sticks her head back in the door once she exits)* Whatever.

Margie roams around in the kitchen looking at things. She picks up a photo of the family and starts to laugh.

MARGIE Oh my God, we were all some silly then. Nice though.

She roams around again and takes the food out of her backpack.

MARGIE *(Pulls back her hair, stretches, runs her hands over her eyes and says to herself)* God, it feels some weird to be here. To be coming back with Mom not here and only Gran. Oh God, I must see what's on the radio. Oh, I loves that song. *(Turns the music up and dances to the song "1970s" by the Smashing Pumpkins)*

The phone rings.

MARGIE Hello … hello, Mom, is that you? Yeah, I'm here at Gran's for the weekend. No, I just got out. Yeah, yeah. The road was fine. Yeah. And the weather's great. Some fog. You know. What? You miss it? The fog? Yeah, right. Whatever. No, she's fine. Well, the same. Grumpy as all hell, but soft around the edges. Yeah. No, I'm fine. Yeah, still in school. Yeah, it's going okay. I'm working at a health food restaurant. Don't laugh. Yeah, actually I loves it. The food and the people that works there. They're from away … Ottawa and Montreal. Yeah, real nice. I think I'm learning more than in university actually. No, I'm not thinking of quitting. I don't think … I dunno. Can we talk about something else? How are you? Yeah, right. Oh, good. And Frank? Good. Ah … Mom … oh … nothing. Yeah, I'm fine. Good. Yeah. No, she's gone to mass. Mrs. Linehan came to pick her up. I'm going to bake us a cake, or something. No, I just feels like being here. Maybe having a chat with her or something. Yeah, I'll tell her you'll call again tomorrow night. Okay, Mom. Okay. Yeah, I'm fine. Yeah. Sure. Okay, bye. *(Hangs up and dials Sophie's number)*

MARGIE Hello, Sophie, how are you? Yeah, I dunno, Sophie. I dunno. It's too big. It's too important. I told you, I gotta get away and think … I don't know … Sophie … I got to go now, Sophie, Gran is home from mass. Okay then, bye, Sophie.

MARGIE Gran, you're back already? Were there many to mass?

GRANDMOTHER Not enough to haul up a punt! Now, you didn't let that fire go down, did you?

MARGIE No, Gran, ah … I don't know, did I? And I didn't bake your cake like I said I would. But I have half a nice one I baked at the restaurant yesterday. We'll have that.

GRANDMOTHER Sure, that's dandy, me dear. We'll have that and a nice cup of tea together. *(Rubs her hands together in anticipation)* Now, you get down the cups and saucers and get the milk and sugar. Tell me, do you still drink that old cow's milk in your tea instead of the tinned?

MARGIE Yeah, as a matter of fact, I do. But, Gran, don't go arguing with me over how I likes my tea, okay? I'm not up to a disagreement tonight.

GRANDMOTHER *(Eyes her suspiciously)* What ails you? Had a spat with the boyfriend?

MARGIE I don't have "the boyfriend," Gran. Everything is not about guys, you know.

GRANDMOTHER Guys? Since when did fellows become guys, I wonder. That's a real American word, that is. Like cookie, and divorce. We never knew guys, never ate a cookie, never had a divorce until the Confederation.

MARGIE Gran, you can't blame everything on Confederation.

GRANDMOTHER *(Dumbfounded)* And why not?

MARGIE They're just words, Gran.

GRANDMOTHER Just words? It seems to me that many a battle was fought over "just words." My, my … did you bake this cake now? *(Tastes cake)*

MARGIE I did. *(Delighted)* Do you like it?

GRANDMOTHER Hmm ... my, my ... that reminds me of an old timey piece of cake, that does. Not too sweet, because there wasn't much sugar to go around. Lots of blueberries because there was always barrels of them. My, my ... I do fancy a bit of cake like that. What else do you cook, besides that green stuff and the rice that's brown?

MARGIE That's brown rice, Gran. It's just the kernel, the husk left on. That's where all the B vitamins are, in the husk.

GRANDMOTHER I remembers when we use to eat the brown bread. Then the white came in, the white flour that we baked with. And then the baker's bread, we called it, the sliced bread. My God, did our work ever get cut down with the sliced bread.

MARGIE Did you like it?

GRANDMOTHER No, but we got use to it. Nothing is better than your own baked bread. Don't tell me you bakes your own bread?

MARGIE I do, but you wouldn't like it. It is whole wheat, organic ... a heavy flour.

GRANDMOTHER That's one thing I can't stand ... *(Flops her hand on table)* being toldt what I don't like. I'll try anything and then I'll say whether I likes it or no. But now this, *(Bites into cake)* this I likes. *(Winks)*

Margie smiles with pride.

MARGIE Mom called.

GRANDMOTHER *(Draws back in disbelief)* Go on!

MARGIE About five minutes after you left.

GRANDMOTHER Oh, right.

MARGIE Gran, she didn't know you weren't here. She didn't plan it. She could have called me in town if she was looking for me. You're so suspicious.

GRANDMOTHER Maybe ... all I knows is we hardly ever talks and when we do it's not for long.

MARGIE She said she'll call back tomorrow, maybe.

GRANDMOTHER Hmm ... maybe ... okay. How about a game of cards? *(Rubs her hands together in excitement)* How about a nice game of 45s?

MARGIE Sure, but you knows I'm not much of a hand at cards.

GRANDMOTHER Yes, I knows, but I'll take you on anyhow. *(Deals out the cards with excitement)*

MARGIE Wasn't there a widower man calling on you for cards last year?

GRANDMOTHER Widower man? You mean ole Charlie O'Reilly? Yeah, I got rid of him right fast too.

MARGIE Why? He seemed harmless and nice even.

GRANDMOTHER Harmless ... yes. Nice ... well, now that's some word, isn't it? Nice. I'd say that saying someone is nice is almost like saying they're invisible. Nice. He's nice. She's nice. It's a nothing word.

MARGIE Well, it gives some kind of description. It means he isn't nasty.

GRANDMOTHER No, he isn't nasty. He's ... nice. Yup ... nice. And looking for a woman to take care of him. I don't want no man in on top of me here ... in a manner of speaking.

MARGIE So ... you want to be alone?

GRANDMOTHER Well, no. I wouldn't mind family. But all men his age wants is someone to cook and clean for them.

MARGIE What about companionship? You'd have someone to play cards with and to eat with.

GRANDMOTHER And to clean up after. No ... not interested.

MARGIE What about Grandfather? You must have cooked and cleaned for him.

GRANDMOTHER For only a couple of months.

MARGIE And then Mom was born. And you a widow.

GRANDMOTHER *(Shifts nervously)* Yeah.

MARGIE So you only had time for one child and then no man to look after.

GRANDMOTHER Mmmm.

MARGIE You never talks much about back then, Gran. How come?

GRANDMOTHER Not much to talk about. Life went on.

MARGIE And Grandfather died. And then Dad drowned. Seems like all the men dies off in this family.

GRANDMOTHER Mmmm ... yeah.

MARGIE *(Sighs)* Guess it's good I don't plan on gettin' married.

GRANDMOTHER Loads of time for that. You're going

to school in order to be independent. Don't be a drain on anyone and then you'll always have your self pride.

MARGIE But, Gran, you never worked ... outside the home, I mean.

GRANDMOTHER I did! I was the only midwife around these parts for years ... till Mrs. Alice came over from North Harbour.

MARGIE I didn't know you were at it all the time. I thought you only helped out like. Now and then.

GRANDMOTHER Well, no. I was at it all the time. Till Lucy come along.

MARGIE A midwife. My God, you must have seen some agony and joy in your day, Gran.

GRANDMOTHER Bit of both. Yeah.

Grandmother shifts uneasily. Margie doesn't notice. She is preoccupied.

MARGIE Gran ... I'm gonna be bold and ask you a question ... a philosophical question. Maybe an ethical one.

GRANDMOTHER A question is still a question, my dear. No matter what fancy clothes you puts on it, so fire away. Nothing can shock me. Except the electric chair and I should be spared that.

MARGIE I have a friend. She's around my age, but a bit older. She has got herself in a bit of a scrape. She's pregnant and he's married and a politician. Kinda high up and kinda older than her. She thinks what she did now ... the affair, was stupid. But she don't know what to do. She's asking my advice all the time and she is my close friend. You don't know her and I knows you don't believe in abortion and I knows you know I'm pro-choice ... that I think a woman should have a right over her own body ...

GRANDMOTHER You always thinks you got me figured out way ahead of time. Slow down. Let's talk about this. So ... she is in the family way without a family. Do she want him?

MARGIE No, not now. She thought she did. She was friggin' obsessed, as a matter of fact. Something about someone being obsessed with someone. To me, that's a sure sign it'll wear off. Too much crammed into the beginning of it.

GRANDMOTHER You're smart there. That's right. If there's a big rush, a big deal, then I'd say it's about more than what's going on.

MARGIE Anyway, Gran ... any advice?

GRANDMOTHER Sounds to me as if she's on the path to your way of thinking.

MARGIE Gran, I don't have any sure way of thinking. I think it's up to the individual person. I just wanted your take on it.

Grandmother gets up, she is flustered. She throws the cards down on the table.

GRANDMOTHER Look, I'm gettin' old. I got no one. No one wants to live here with me. I'd say it's the home for me ... or worse. And I don't want that. I don't want to be around a crowd of old, sick people like myself. I can't help it. I knows it's selfish. *(She sits in her rocker, rocks furiously and becomes very agitated.)*

MARGIE Gran, what's wrong? I was only talking about my friend, someone you don't even know. I was only asking your opinion, since I told her I'd let her know mine, and I just don't know how I think. I thought that since you and me were talking that you'd be able to help.

GRANDMOTHER I can't help with such a thing. I got my religion.

MARGIE And is it a help, your religion?

GRANDMOTHER It was. It is. Yes, it is still. Look, we're born, we lives this life, we makes mistakes. We thinks we does the best we can do. *(She runs her hands though Margie's hair, while Margie kneels by the rocker.)* Oh child … I feels shockin' tormented. I have been all these years. And now … now I … I have to … I have to take things a step at a time.

MARGIE Gran, what's the matter with you? God in heaven, I've never seen you like this. What is it?

GRANDMOTHER Now look, I'm going to tell you something and you got to promise me you won't go runnin' to Lucy. Promise? Promise!

MARGIE Gran, what is it? You're scaring me.

GRANDMOTHER I got to tell someone. I can't keep keeping it inside of me. I got no one to turn to.

MARGIE Gran … *(Pleads)*

GRANDMOTHER I was to the doctor's a couple of months back. I had tests because I was having pain.

MARGIE Gran, this is not good, is it? I can tell. Oh, Gran.

GRANDMOTHER Look, child. Life deals up what it deals. Now, I'm telling you because you're here with me and someone has to know sooner or later. And we're close, so I feels okay to tell you, although it's hard.

MARGIE You tell me, Gran. I'm not saying the word. It's that word, isn't it?

GRANDMOTHER It is, my dear. It is.

MARGIE Where?

GRANDMOTHER Well, a couple of places. Big places. Liver, bowel, lung. And travelling, they say. On the move.

MARGIE Oh, Gran. *(Grabs her knees and throws her head on her lap)* Gran ... stop. Turn back the time. It's not true. Is it?

GRANDMOTHER Everything is changed now, isn't it? I knew that would happen. I knew the minute I started talking about it everything would change. The world would never be the same for me. But it's said now. And now more than me have to deal with it. I'm sorry, Margie honey.

MARGIE Gran ... we got to tell Mom and Junior and ... and ...

GRANDMOTHER In time. In time. Let's just take this a step at a time for now. All I knows is that I'm not alone. All up and down this shore there's a string of us. Like a string of pearls, only it is tarnished pearls. There's Phonse with it in his bones and his throat. Charlie with bowel and stomach. Pat with bowel. Alice with bowel. Tony with bowel. Mick with bowel and stomach. Johnny with brain. Pete with brain. Arnold with brain. The list is endless. One time it was all the TB. All different now.

MARGIE But you've been to the doctors. They must be saying something. Something to be done.

GRANDMOTHER Nothing. I tell you, nothing. Three months, they say, me dear. Three short months. Or maybe three long months.

MARGIE I'm calling Mom right now.

GRANDMOTHER You are doing no such thing. You hear me? I confided in you. Don't you go break that. Not now. Not right now. You hear me, Margie? Don't I have some say here?

MARGIE Gran, then when? I need to talk to Mom. Mom needs to know.

GRANDMOTHER Yes, in time. But not now. You and me, we got a lot more talking to do first.

Lights fade and come up again slowly. Margie is sitting at the kitchen table. Grandmother is serving tea. Margie looks dumbstruck.

MARGIE And so you took her and reared her and … and … never said a word.

Grandmother looks at Margie while stirring sugar in her tea.

GRANDMOTHER What was there to say? In my day you didn't talk to children. Now it's all different. Everyone talks to everyone else about everything. Not in my day though.

MARGIE But you let her grow up not knowing.

GRANDMOTHER Not knowing. Not knowing what? I thought if I told her I might be inviting trouble. You know, it could have set her off on some kind of quest. It would have disturbed her whole childhood.

MARGIE But it was all false. Her whole childhood was a dupe.

GRANDMOTHER A dupe! I beg to differ there, as the old folks used to say. I never duped anyone! If something is done with the best regard for the other, then how is that a dupe? I wasn't getting any advantage out of it. Your mother's real mother was beyond caring for a child. And she didn't have two cents to rub together. I'll tell you the truth now, I don't even know if young Nancy even knew she had her.

MARGIE Nancy ... my grandmother's name was Nancy. Not Nan. Not you!

GRANDMOTHER *(Crestfallen)* That slights. But I can take it. I do understand.

MARGIE Oh, Gran, I'm sorry. Here I am talking about me and it's you that needs tending to.

GRANDMOTHER I do not. And when I do, I'll get it in style at the hospital, I expect. Child, I had to tell you. I had to let the family know before ...

MARGIE What did you mean when you said that Mom's real mother was beyond caring for a child?

GRANDMOTHER She was ... well ... slow, I suppose you'd say. Somewhat backward, young for her age.

MARGIE Delayed, you mean?

GRANDMOTHER Well, I suppose. I don't know. They keeps changing the name of it, I suppose, to protect them from the labels.

MARGIE Who were her family? And how come she had a baby?

GRANDMOTHER Her family were all died off, from sickness. She was an orphan, took care of by an old aunt. She had your mother because ... because ... she was taken advantage of.

MARGIE Do you know by who or whom?

GRANDMOTHER He's dead now. And that family wasn't nice.

MARGIE So I come from a long line of mentally delayed and criminals, is that it?

GRANDMOTHER Her family, Nancy's, were good people and not retarded at all. I don't know what happened with Nancy. She could have been dropped or something.

MARGIE Dropped ... on her head like?

GRANDMOTHER I don't know. Could have. It happens. Happened a lot then, I think.

MARGIE God, Gran ...

GRANDMOTHER I know, I know. It is a lot to have slung at you in the one day. Should we call it a day then? *(Starts to get up and heads towards the bedroom slowly)*

MARGIE Yeah, we'll call it a day. A long one. I have a lot to think about. It makes me feel like Mom is all alone up there in Alberta.

GRANDMOTHER Well, you just thinks that because you feels alone and you knows a secret. Good night, now, me dear. Don't be up brooding long. You're alive and healthy, and that's the main thing.

MARGIE Yeah, Gran. And Gran ... thanks for telling me ... everything.

Lights fade as Grandmother exits. Margie sits on the couch and the lights soften around her.

MARGIE Holy God! What a day! My head feels ready to burst. First Sophie, now this. Sophie is mild compared to this. My gran ain't really my gran, and she's dying of cancer. Oh God, there's so much going on. *(Lights fade as Margie pulls the baseball cap down over her face and yawns. Music plays.)*

Lights up after the music has been playing for a while. Grandmother enters with her nightgown on and a cup in her hand. She stares at Margie sleeping on the couch.

GRANDMOTHER She still does that. Falls asleep on the couch no matter how much she says she won't. Just like a little girl, she is, still. Oh my ... she's had a hard day of it. But not a hard life all the same. If Lucy had been reared by Nancy ... well, she couldn't be reared. It would have been foster homes. I was never a foster home. I saw a job that needed to be done and I did it. Thanks be to God Lucy was all right. I watched for signs. I was frightened to death. Didn't know if I could rear a simple child. But Lucy was always sharp as a tack. Always wanting to advance herself. Got her hair dressing certificate, even kept at it after she married. Is a good thing she did, I suppose, 'cause when Pad drowned she had that to support her. I dreads the thought of Lucy knowing ... about herself and about my illness. Oh my, I've no pain ... yet, thanks be to God. I just pray the Lord takes me fast is all. *(Sits in her rocker and starts to snore as she dozes off)*

MARGIE *(In her sleep)* I'm okay Sophie ... just confused. No, I don't want you to not have the baby. No, I'll help you. I'm sure, yes. We'll rear it together. No. Yes, I'm sure.

GRANDMOTHER *(In her sleep)* No, Henry, no, I said to him. I'm rearing that child whether you likes it or not. It was you who done it to her ... to poor Nancy. So it's the least I can do for your sins. I'm not doing it to help you, Henry ... no way. I'm doing it for the child ... I'm doing it for the child.

MARGIE *(In her sleep)* Sophie, I don't care. I'll tell Mom. I'll tell Gran. I'll tell the world. We'll raise this child in peace and love. That's not romantic. That's the truth. We'll give this child a home, the two of us.

GRANDMOTHER *(In her sleep)* And one thing I'll tell you right now, Henry. You'll not share my bed another night after what you done. And you've no right to call yourself a Christian. And don't blame it on the liquor. It is your black soul done that and I banish you. You and your darkness. Banish! Banish! Go! Get! *(Wakes herself and Margie up)*

MARGIE What! What's going on!

GRANDMOTHER What! What's going on!

MARGIE Gran! Gran! For God's sake, Gran. You were ravin'. You were carrying on in your sleep. Calling out.

GRANDMOTHER *(Wipes drool from the side of her mouth)* I was not. That was you. You were talking in your sleep. I heard you.

MARGIE I was not. I was asleep.

GRANDMOTHER Yes, and talking. Talking your troubles. I heard you.

MARGIE Gran, you were asleep. I knows you were. I can tell when you sleeps. I heard you snoring in my sleep. I mean in your sleep. *(Wipes her eyes and is confused)*

GRANDMOTHER Oh no. I haven't had that sign in years. Oh my, what does that mean now? I was asleep, maybe. And I heard you talking in your sleep. Did you hear me talking in mine?

MARGIE I ... I don't know ... I ... I ... had the strangest dream. All mixed up. You were in it and my ... my ... friend Sophie was in it. And ye were talking. Ye were saying that some bad man did something, but that it'd be all right because the two of us were going to take care of it. Oh God, I don't know what I'm saying. Look, Gran, I got something to talk about to you.

GRANDMOTHER Hold on a minute. Hold on. You don't understand. You see, the gift was handed down and it skipped generations. That's what I heard. The old people used to say that the gift was brought over from the back hills of the county Tipperary. Only amongst the women, as far as I know. Certain ones could read each other's dreams. If they were close, or if great troubles were hanging over them. Margie, I came in here, into this room, and you were asleep on the couch and I spoke out loud my thoughts and then I fell asleep. I knows I dreamt. I knows because I feels rested. Like after a powerful night's sleep. And only dreams does that to me.

MARGIE Gran, you're spookin' me out. Stop it. What's all this about reading each other's dreams? We're not even family, I mean, with all due respect, Gran. You said it was handed down, so how could it have been if you aren't really my grandmother?

GRANDMOTHER *(Muddled)* Well, well, oh my, it is a tangled web, my dear. My husband, your false grand-father was really your real grandfather. I'm not real at all. I'm the only one that's not real at all. I'm the only real stranger here in this family.

MARGIE Gran! Gran! For God's sake, Gran, you're making me dizzy. My false grandfather, what the hell does that mean? My false grandfather is my real … grandpa … sounds like that song … I'm my own grandpa. Jesus, what is going on?

GRANDMOTHER Now listen. And listen close, because I'm not going over this again. Your grandfather … my husband … he was a son of a … he was beyond hope. I didn't know it when I married him. He was a hard worker, that's all I knew. He and I, well, we never hit it off in the honeymoon suite, if you know what I means. There was something about him. Well, I found out what that something was. Kind of slimy, he was. It wasn't my fault we didn't hit it off. I was never one for blaming myself when the blame didn't belong to me. No, he was the way he was … and that was that.

MARGIE Gran! What way was he, for God's sake?

GRANDMOTHER He went after that poor little thing … young Nancy. He got her in the family way and I took over the baby, his responsibility, because I knew that if I didn't, he wouldn't care. And then I banished him. I reared Lucy, your mother, like me own, even though she wasn't. But I was too embarrassed to tell you the real father earlier. You got that through my dream.

MARGIE I did not! You just told me. Gran, you're so superstitious.

GRANDMOTHER That's not superstition. That's old times … that's the gift. You'll be thankful someday, even if it isn't blood passed it on to you.

MARGIE Sounds like the blood on my side is pretty damn dirtied.

GRANDMOTHER But the hands that reared you are clean. I can promise you that.

MARGIE (*Goes to the rocker and lays her head on Grandmother's lap*) Gran, don't I know that. I don't know a better soul than you. You are my grandmother. I'm adopting you, Gran.

GRANDMOTHER (*Pats her head*) Fair enough, since I already adopted your mother, so then I suppose you're able to adopt me right back.

MARGIE Gran, can I call Mom? And just tell her, you know, tell her about you? Your health?

GRANDMOTHER Or lack of it? I suppose, girl. We can't keep all these secrets stored up forever. They'll kill us. *(Lights fade. Music starts playing for awhile. Grandmother exits.)*

Lights up on Margie playing solitaire at table. Lucy enters. She is carrying a suitcase. She places it on the floor, looks around and sighs. She slumps her shoulders. Margie looks up from her game and puts out her cigarette.

LUCY What? You smoking? You, the health freak?

MARGIE Mom, oh, Mom. Come here to me. *(They embrace and cry. Lights fade.)*

Lights up on Margie and Lucy sitting at the table having a cup of tea.

LUCY Holy Christ! Am I in a soap opera, or what?

MARGIE Mom, soap operas get their information from real life, not vice versa.

LUCY Oh, so most normal family situations has stuff like this going on? Have I been on a retreat for forty years or something?

MARGIE Mom, Gran is sick.

LUCY Yeah, but not my real ma, and not your real grandma ... right? Help me out here. This is frightfully new to me, girl.

MARGIE Mom ... let's just call her Gran, okay? Gran got less than a month, by the way she's fadin', Mom. And like I toldt you on the phone, no, she's not my real grandma nor your ma, but she is who she is and she's dying ... okay?

LUCY *(Rubs her feet)* Look, Margie, I know what you're saying, but give me a bit of time, would you? Just give me a cup of tea and a bit of time to absorb all this.

MARGIE Absorb away, Mom. I got nothing but time.
Which is more than I can say for Gran.

LUCY Oh, that's precious. Am I supposed to feel guilty
here? Over something I had no part in? That's precious.
I'll contemplate over that now while I'm trying to figure
out who my real mother was.

MARGIE Mom, I hate to be the one to tell you, but this
isn't about us right now. Maybe later it will be, but right
now this woman who reared us is dying, so what are we
going to do about it?

LUCY Fair enough. So ... who exactly is my real
mother?

MARGIE Nancy, from under the bridge.

LUCY Is that the name of a folksong or something, or
is it really the name of my mother? "Nancy ... from in
under the bridge."

MARGIE Actually, I said, "Nancy from under the
bridge," not "Nancy from in under the bridge," but
whatever.

LUCY Yes, indeed ... whatever.

MARGIE It's probably both, a folksong and your
mother. Anyway, Nancy was a Hayes, from the next
cove up. And Nan don't know if she was dropped or if it
is genetic. I'm sorry to be so blasé, but I'm bone-tired.

LUCY Dropped or patterned. No consolation either
way. The thing is ... how am I supposed to look at her ...
I mean upon her? As my mother or my saviour? She
helped out in a big way, there's no doubt about that.

MARGIE Gran was ahead of her time in some ways. I mean, she saw how one kind of family didn't work, so she designed another. Really, she was ahead of the whole game, just like her generation was ahead of it with the perfect diet ... the macrobiotic diet.

LUCY Margie, Margie, Margie, honey ... my feet are killing me and my mind is boggled. Could you please talk the macro later? Does Mother know I'm here?

MARGIE No, she don't.

LUCY Is she resting comfortably?

MARGIE The nurses says she's the best patient they ever had. Whatever that means.

LUCY Could mean she's no trouble, but I can't imagine Mom no trouble to anyone.

MARGIE She's lost her edge ... a bit.

LUCY Oh my, lost her edge ... that's too much to contemplate.

Door opens and Grandmother enters slowly.

MARGIE Gran! You were supposed to ring that bell when you wanted to get up, so I could help you.

GRANDMOTHER Well, Margie honey ... I guess I didn't need help then, did I? We have a visitor. Is it our Lucy then?

LUCY *(Uncomfortable for a minute, but goes to her)* Mom, Mom ... why didn't you tell us sooner?

GRANDMOTHER And have ye moping after me? Have ye getting on my nerves and under me feet? Not likely.

LUCY I'd have come sooner.

GRANDMOTHER But you're here now. That's the main thing.

LUCY Yes, that's the main thing.

GRANDMOTHER Margie, did you get your mother a cup of tea? All the young crowd knows now is coffee *(Spoken in a grand accent)* and the beer parlours. In my day it was a drop of wine Christmas, along with the little bottles of French perfume from St. Peter's. And in your day, Lucy, you'd never go out to a dance without a man, or a crowd of girls to pal up with. Not young Margie here. She knows the coffee shops and the beer parlours all on her own.

LUCY What's wrong with young women being independent, Mother? Why wait for a man for your every move?

GRANDMOTHER Oh, I waited for no man for nothing. If I did, I'd still be sittin' on the doorstep twiddling my thumbs, and I was never one for to wait for nothing. *(She stumbles and they rush to her.)* Oh my ... what was that? Like a flash of light up through my middle. Whew! That must be how the Holy Spirit entered wasisname.

LUCY Sit down, Mother. Here, pour up that tea, Margie.

GRANDMOTHER A bit of that painkiller wouldn't go astray right now either. Over there in the cupboard, Margie. That's the girl.

LUCY Mother, you should be in the bed. Come on, I'll help you back.

GRANDMOTHER No, Lucy. I can't spend all me time

in the bed. I'm not give up to the bed yet. That time will come when it comes. But while I got a leg to stand on ... to hell with the bed!

LUCY No change in you, Mother. Sickness or no sickness, you're still as feisty as ever.

MARGIE *(Gives Grandmother her pill)* Here, Gran, take that and relax a bit now.

Grandmother takes the pill, settles back and looks from Margie to Lucy and back again.

GRANDMOTHER *(To Margie)* You toldt her! You toldt her, didn't you?

MARGIE Wha? You're sick. Yeah, *(Shifts uneasily)* of course I toldt her.

GRANDMOTHER That's not what I mean and you knows it. *(Looks at Lucy)*

LUCY Yeah, I knows. It's all right, Margie. Mother, I'm glad Margie told me.

GRANDMOTHER Yeah, well I'm not. I wanted to talk about all this with you myself. Between the two of us. I let the cat out of the bag, so to speak, because I was upset about this damn cancer. I got upset and it all spilled out.

LUCY It's all right, Mother ...

Grandmother cuts her off.

GRANDMOTHER You don't have to call me that. You're under no obligation ...

LUCY What am I supposed to call you? Regina? I can't go calling you by your first name now, or Mrs. ...

MARGIE And you can't call her what I calls her …
Gran. And I don't know what else to call you.

*Margie walks over to the couch and lies down with a magazine
up to her face.*

LUCY Oh, I don't care what anybody calls anybody!
You reared me so to hell with it. You're my mother,
Mother. I just wants to know the story is all. Nancy-
under-the-bridge was my real mother, or Nancy-in-under-
the-bridge, or whatever, and … and … your real
husband … was my real father? Help me out here,
Mother, am I correct?

GRANDMOTHER Yes, my real husband was a real
bas … was your real father. But I banished him. He
wasn't worth being called a husband, let alone a father.

LUCY So where is he now?

GRANDMOTHER Six feet under. When I banished
him he turned into a drunk, but he wasn't far from it
before he met me. He was born a drunk and he died a
drunk. Set fire to hisself in the bed when he was loaded.
At least he never got his hands on no more innocents.

LUCY So my … mother … was an innocent?

GRANDMOTHER As a lamb.

LUCY And by innocent … you mean …

GRANDMOTHER I means innocent! The girl never
did no harm to no one.

MARGIE That's a lot of double negatives there, Gran.
(Magazine down here)

Lucy and Grandmother look at her questioningly.

MARGIE *(To Lucy)* Gran is always correcting my

English, or my Irish, as she calls it. Even though it's English. I'm just telling her that she can't use two negatives like "Never did no harm to no one" ... like. Okay, forget it. Just remember that the next time you corrects me, Gran, okay? Or was that three negatives? Okay, okay, forget it. *(Magazine back up to face)*

LUCY Where in the name of God were we?

GRANDMOTHER Your ... mother.

LUCY My God, Mother, it's so strange to hear you say someone else was my mother besides you. I mean I can't fathom it yet.

GRANDMOTHER *(Takes Lucy's hands in her own)* Lucy, when I saw what went on I stepped in. I found out what happened to young Nancy. She toldt it right innocent like one day when the women were out on the berry grounds. She said it as if she made no more a pass on it than sneezing. But that wasn't her fault. And her old aunt was there, old Mrs. Mary, and old Mrs. Mary screeched and tore at her hair and said, "I knew," she said. "I knew Nancy was in trouble. I watched her monthlies." Oh God in heaven, she bawled out to me and she flung all her berries out of her bucket at me, and she wailed and tore at me. I took her by the wrists and I said, "Now, Mrs. Mary, stop it, stop it now," I said. "I knows what your Nancy is saying is true. I knows it be- cause I knows that bastard I married isn't fit for this earth. But it wasn't me who done it, Mrs. Mary. It wasn't me, but I'm willing to take charge here, and I'm willing to be responsible where he can't because he's useless. Be- lieve me, we're all better off without him darkening our doors." And Mrs. Mary said, "You'd kick him out?" And I said, "After this bit of news ... yes. He's gone. And I'll stay with young Nancy and I'll birth her baby and I'll rear it, Mrs. Mary," I said. "You have my word. If that be your will." Well, she grabbed a holdt to me and she looked me square in the eye, there on the barrens, and she said, "You do that. You do that, or else I'll haunt you night and day." So I done it. Ole Mrs. Mary even came to live with me. You remember her?

LUCY Yes, yes I do. With the rosary beads always in her hands and she spoke the Gaelic when she prayed, didn't she? She was my relative, Mrs. Mary?

GRANDMOTHER Yes, as far as that goes, she was. The Lord rest her.

LUCY And Nancy died giving birth to me?

GRANDMOTHER Yes, that's right. God rest her soul. You were born at eight o'clock in the morning. I remember we had a hard night of it. Nancy was in a bad way, and right towards the end a bird flew into the room where we had the window up to give her air. And I crossed myself and I knew. A bird in the house meant either her or you.

LUCY And it was her.

GRANDMOTHER And it was her.

All three sit silently for a while.

LUCY My father was your husband.

GRANDMOTHER That's right.

LUCY And he took advantage of my mother, who was an innocent.

GRANDMOTHER Yes.

LUCY *(Sighs)* And she died bringing me into the world, and my father died from drink.

GRANDMOTHER Yes.

LUCY And would you have told me, if you hadn't of gotten sick?

GRANDMOTHER Yes.

LUCY When?

GRANDMOTHER This coming Christmas.

LUCY Christmas? Some gift.

GRANDMOTHER The gift of truth.

LUCY Why not the truth from the beginning?

GRANDMOTHER I was afraid it would mark you.

LUCY Mark me? I'd say I was already marked, wouldn't you?

GRANDMOTHER It was not the best possible beginning, but it was not as bad as some had it.

LUCY Part of me don't care. Isn't that funny? Part of me accepts it and ... why do I feel so ... so solid?

Margie puts down her magazine, looks at them.

MARGIE Because you had a good bringing up. Even if Gran was ornery sometimes.

GRANDMOTHER What? Me?

LUCY Margie's right, Mother. I did have a good upbringing. You stuck to me like glue, even if I wanted you to back off sometimes. You were always there.

GRANDMOTHER You were no trouble to rear. You were always good. If stubborn.

MARGIE Wonder where she gets that?

GRANDMOTHER That child got an answer for everything.

LUCY She's hardly a child anymore. All growed up and living in St. John's.

MARGIE So, Mom, me and my girlfriend Sophie have decided to raise her baby together.

LUCY How?

MARGIE One will get a job while the other minds the baby. We'll take turns.

LUCY Margie, why are you taking this on?

MARGIE Because I believe it is the right thing to do. To help someone in need ... and ... I love her.

LUCY Don't Sophie have family to help her?

MARGIE No, the thing is, Mom, she don't. She's all alone in the world. She's adopted, from up north, and her parents don't want no part of it. Said she made her bed ... so much for Christian love.

LUCY And you feels responsible?

MARGIE No! Well, yes, but I also believe in Sophie, Mom. I believe she is the best one to rear her baby ... with help.

GRANDMOTHER She could be right, Lucy. She could be very right.

LUCY But what about university? I thought you wanted to get your education.

MARGIE I do ... but not right now. I already toldt you I was learning more at the health food restaurant than I am in school. Maybe I'm meant to be a cook or own a business. They tells me at the restaurant I'm a good hand at both.

GRANDMOTHER Oh, she's a keen hand to cook, Lucy. Even if the stuff is strange, it still tastes good. Some lot of flavour to it.

LUCY So you and Sophie will rear this baby, taking turns at work?

MARGIE And school. Sophie wants to be a writer. She's already a good writer. She's a good person, Mom.

LUCY Oh, I've no doubt, if she's your friend. You were always sensible, honey. It just seems a lot to take on. Maybe you got your head in the clouds.

MARGIE Mom, if there's a problem comes along with doing this, then I'll talk to you. I'll keep the lines of communication open. Gran taught me to do that from now on.

GRANDMOTHER Glad to be good for something finally. I'm feeling a little queer in the head now, fuzzy. Can you help me to bed now, girls?

Lucy and Margie get up to help her.

LUCY Now, Mother, you ask our help more often from now on.

GRANDMOTHER It might come to that. And sooner than we thinks.

Lights fade as all three exit.

FIRST VIEW OF THE SEA

Approximately 50 minutes

First View of the Sea was produced in 2007 in the Cuslett Community Arts Centre.

Mother and her grown son live together in the family home. Mother is struggling with the early stages of dementia. She confuses her need to talk about the past, the old ways of living, the superstitions and genealogy, with this dementia. The son is interested in exploring all this with her, but the daughter, who lives in the city, thinks that the son is making the dementia worse. The tension among all three is oft times fraught with humour as well as pathos. Family members learn as they go along that they are never too old to learn about each other.

LIST OF CHARACTERS & ACTORS (2007 PRODUCTION)

MOTHER: Mildred Dohey
TOMMY: Paul Rowe
ANGELA: Connie Newhook

SCENE ONE

*Lights up on kitchen with woodstove, table, chairs, etc., and
bed off to one side with old woman turned to wall, back to
audience.*

MOTHER What? Is that you? What do you want?
Who the hell are you? What? Oh yes. Is that right? Sure,
I'm not afraid of you. You were here last night, right?
Am I right? Ha! Righto, buddy boy! *(Pause)* Wait. Wait.
(She reaches out and then falls back on her bed.) Ah, hell's
flames on you! Go! Get! *(Lights down)*

*Lights up. Son enters the kitchen with an armload of wood.
He is wearing jeans, a lumber jacket, a toque and gloves. He
lays the wood down in the woodbox by the woodstove and
checks the fire. He moves the kettle over the flames. He takes
off his gloves and coat. He sits down in a chair by stove and
pushes the toque to back of his head. He takes a sliver from
the wood and picks his teeth with it, takes his time, nods and
scratches his head. On the other side of the partition Mother
is turning in the blankets. The audience only sees the blankets
move. There is a big grunt. She heaves the blankets off and
swings legs over side of bed. She is very old. She scratches her
head and groans.*

MOTHER Ah … oh my. Where is he? *(Reaches for stick
that leans against the bed and bangs it against the floor)*

*Son is still picking his teeth. He stops for a moment when he
hears the stick, but then goes back to picking teeth.*

MOTHER Tommy, Tommy … are you there, or where
are you? I could be dead. I could be dead.

SON *(Gets up and starts to get the food ready)* The kettle is
boiled. I'll bring it to you … *(Pauses)* di-rect-ly. *(Spoken
with exaggeration and a laugh)*

MOTHER Humph! Who's out there with you at this
hour?

SON The usual crowd. My harem. My bevy of beauties.

MOTHER You mind the priest don't walk in on you with that crowd in. You hear me? Am I not good enough for an introduction, or what?

SON I'll be there the once. You can meet them all then. Betty, Mary, Laurie and Ann. Then there's Helen and Hortense and Alice and Pretense. Or is it Prudence? Dear Prudence, won't you come out to play? *(Sings)*

MOTHER Where's my tea I'm asking you? It's trying to starve me, you are.

Son is making tea and toast. He puts it on a tray, along with butter, jam, milk and sugar. He goes to her bedroom, pulls up a chair and puts the tray on it. He pulls over another chair and sits down.

SON Here it is now. Nice and hot for you!

MOTHER I have to say me grace first. Had that visitor again last night.

SON Which one?

MOTHER There's only one.

SON At a time ... but there's more than one.

MOTHER Not to me. Must be that crowd goes to you you're talking about.

SON You has a woman sometimes ... your mother. And then there was the man the one time.

MOTHER It was the man. There was only half of him.

SON What half?

MOTHER The top. But he never talked ... or yes he did.

SON You going eating that?

MOTHER I might. You want it? Go on.

SON No, you go on. Eat it. That's good jam. Mrs. O'Reilly made that for you, remember?

MOTHER Mrs. O'Reilly who? She's dead.

SON No, the one that's alive.

MOTHER She's dead. You eat that. Eat half. I'll eat the rest.

SON You first. Did he speak to you?

MOTHER Who?

SON Buddy.

MOTHER What came?

SON Yes, him.

MOTHER Something ... he said something about his clean shirt. I don't know ... don't confuse me.

SON I'm not confusing you. I'm only asking. You were saying ...

MOTHER I was not. I was not saying. I'm going back to sleep for a spell. It's too early yet.

SON You're going back to sleep, are ya? That's all you're eating? That's not much. Not enough to keep a nit alive.

MOTHER To keep a bird alive.

SON What?

MOTHER You're always changing everything. It's "eat enough to keep a bird alive." How am I supposed to know what you're talking about? Trying to confuse me, see?

SON I only does that to entertain myself. To keep myself from climbing on the ceiling.

MOTHER See! Climbing the walls, it is. See!

Son stands up to take tray away.

SON What do you want for your lunch? More of the same? How about a nice soft-boiled egg?

MOTHER I don't care. I don't care what you brings me. I could be dead by then. But you wouldn't know. You'd never know.

SON Well, I'd find out sooner or later. There'd be a strong smell … eventually.

MOTHER There's not as many dead on the go as there used to be. Where are all the dead to?

SON Buried and in their graves. If they're good dead.

MOTHER One time, they'd be all over the place. Roaming in the hills in the dark. There's no dark anymore, is the thing.

SON Well, there's night. That's dark.

MOTHER Not dark like it was once. Lights everywhere now. On all the time. No wonder the government got no money.

SON Oh, they got money. They spends it on keeping the lights on in the dark so the money don't get stoldt.

MOTHER If they kept the lights off, no one'd know where the money was to.

SON You should be in the government. We'd all be better off.

MOTHER I could have got a good job. If I'd of got past the third book. But she hauled me out of school at ten years old. There was no laws then.

SON There was laws. Ever since Charles Dickens …

MOTHER Who is he? He wasn't out around the bay when I was growing up, whoever he was.

SON He brought it up that children were being used as chimney sweeps on account of their being so small they could fit down the chimneys.

MOTHER What? He never had to turn fish till his back gave out though, did he?

SON No place to turn fish in London.

MOTHER London? What? The queen is never on television anymore. I used to love seeing her on the television telling us to be good and that everything'd be all right. There's no one talking like that anymore. Except the priest do be.

SON Hmm … they can talk like that all right. Nothing to worry about, see?

MOTHER Nothing to worry about? Mind now. They got the world to worry about. My God, b'y, what do you know? The responsibilities on their shoulders. You couldn't fathom it. *(Turns in to the wall)*

SON You're enough responsibility for me. Now tell me what you wants for your lunch so you don't go complaining.

MOTHER Nothing. What odds what I eats? Hen scratch. I don't care.

SON We got no hens. *(Exits)*

MOTHER Humph! Ah ... the devil scald you.
(Lights fade)

SCENE TWO
Lights up on bed.

MOTHER Why shouldn't I be mad? I am goddamned
mad. I got nothing but time, and not much of that. Time.
Time. Time. Great big gaping hole of time. A big, deep,
black well of it. Grand stretch of sky of it. Time everywhere except ahead. *(Yells)* How old am I? *(No response)*
No, no fear anyone'd be around. There was never anyone
around to take care of me and there's still not. Why is it all
up to me? Is that you? *(Looks straight ahead. No response)*
You! What are you at here again? I never asked you. Why
can't Father come again? The once only. And you standing
there as if you were welcome. I never asked for you. You
were never there when I was trying to grow up. What do
you want now? Why don't you say anything? Ya goddamn
thing. Do you hear that? What kind of a mother are you?
Leaving your children to fend for ourselves so you could
marry fat ole Phonse Lundrigan. And Father not cold.
And Father so handsome. To go from such a cut of a man
to a great blob of whale blubber. What was that? Times
were hard. Oh, yeah. When were they not? Don't give me
that. You were all for the mirror and the wallet, you were.
A dance in Rushoon and you were gone straight away.
The priest wouldn't be docked and you were on the dance
floor. Brazen, no not brazen, that's not the word for you,
because you were thoughtless. More like numb. Or what
the hell were you? Ah, what odds now? Where's he to?
Tommy! He don't give a good goddamn. The whole
crowd were like that. Your crowd and then my crowd. But
no one could say that about me. No. No way. I let things
bother me too much, is my problem. Why is everything
such a god-blessed fight? Why is it so hard to get your
own way now and again? Why? What?

SCENE THREE

Lights up on kitchen and fade on bedroom. Son is looking out the window with his legs crossed and his foot beating out a silent rhythm. The phone rings.

SON Hello. Oh pretty good. Yourself? *(Sits back down at the window)*

Lights up on Mother.

MOTHER Can't breathe in this town. How did I get here? I landed here. Landed. On the go. Always on the go. Since I was ten years old. Worked out. I'm worked out. But I'd work yet if I could. I would. There was Meersheen, Isle Valen, Marystown, Little Harbour and Clattice Harbour. Every harbour! Rushoon, Placentia and St. John's. Oh my God! I'm bet out just remembering them all. And the tide coming in the gut and moving up the arm. All the body parts. The tide pushing the eels up the arm that swum all the way from Norway or that swims all the way back to Norway, whichever what way it is. Those arms of water cutting through the town and cutting out again. Day in, day out. And the mountains, or is it a hill, stuck in the middle, always stuck there. Water always moving. In. Out. Good for drowning cats though! Get rid of the kittens in a brin bag. But one morning I tossed them out with the tide and they came back again on the evening tide. Young fellow over the way saw me doing it and came to the door with the soppin' wet bag, saying, "Here you go, missus, the bag of cats you almost drowned."

Lights back up on Son singing "Waterloo. Waterloo. How will you meet your Waterloo?"

MOTHER Uncle Charlie used to sing that song. No, not that American one. The old, old one about Napoleon Bonaparte marching into Moscow. And it being in a blaze … and he lost the bonny bunch of roses oh … *(She* *sings this last part.)* Cute? There's no counting his cutenesses. *(She shouts out.)* Any newses?

SON That was Ange.

MOTHER What was?

SON What was on the phone. She's coming out from town.

MOTHER Maybe.

SON I'm only telling you.

MOTHER Yes, well … are you bringing me my breakfast now?

SON I would. If it was breakfast time. It's handier to lunchtime now.

MOTHER Time. Time. What's that got to do with my hunger?

SON *(Distracted from other room)* Righto!

MOTHER It was hard on her to lose Joseph. We all know that. And he so strong and good. A good worker. Only eighteen years old too. The young woman from town came out on a holiday, she was the magistrate's niece and she took to Patsy, wanted to pal around with Patsy, so off they went and went swimming. And they got in trouble in the water, the current got too strong and Patsy yelled out to Joseph. He was up on the hill making hay. It was August month and he saw the young woman go under as he ran and jumped from the hill into the sea, and he swum to Patsy and told her to float herself while he went after the young woman. But the current got the both of them. Another man saw it all and got to Patsy in time, just barely in time. The magistrate and the young woman's family, they were afeared we'd blame them, on account of Joseph losing his life trying to save her, but what would be the good of that? Blame. Regret, yes, of course, or something like it, but Joseph only done what any person would do. Any decent person. Time for the litany now. Time to remember all the things before they're forgot. The cure for the toothache – take a rock off Father Martin's gravesite, or drive a horse nail into a tree that will never be cut down. Arthritis – wear an aluminium ring, or al-yoo-min-ee-em, as grandfather used to say. Nosebleed – put a cold rock on the back of your neck. Sore eyes – May snow melted. Sore throat – hot salt flattened out in a brown paper bag, place it in a woollen sock and tie it around your throat. Water boils – nine doubles of grey woollen thread wrapped around your wrist and say Father, Son and Holy Ghost. Cuts – put flour in the cut and wrap it up, or cover the cut with turpentine and wrap it up. Headache – tie a band tight around your head. And if you've leg cramps, make the sign of the cross with your boots. *(She makes the sign of the cross with her arms held high.)*

MOTHER Up the line there, up the line, they buried their unwanted children under the trees. You don't believe me? Go check. *(Her back is turned to audience as she faces the wall. Long silence)*

MOTHER An' everybody says to me, they says, "Sure, Mrs. Flynn, you don't look your age, no way." An' Helen there, a year younger than me, and I look like the younger one. True! That's true! That's what they all says to me. I'm only saying.

SCENE FOUR
Lights up on kitchen, Mother sitting on bed, turned to wall, back to audience.

SON Angela is on her way out from town.

MOTHER Angela who?

SON Angela, your daughter.

MOTHER Where's she to?

SON St. John's.

MOTHER Not Florida? Not New York?

SON No, that's Patsy. And Molly. Ree-spect-tif-lee. *(Same drawn out way he said 'directly' before)*

MOTHER The Americans.

SON That'd be them.

MOTHER If Candlemas Day is clear and fine, the rest of winter is left behind. If Candlemas Day is rough and grum, there's more of winter yet to come.

SON Whatever.

MOTHER February 2nd. Celebrated every year by the Holy Mother Catholic Church of God.

SON The Vatican. Rome. Italy. The planet Earth.

MOTHER Don't start.

SON February 2nd. That was Dad's birthday, wasn't it? And don't say 'Dad who?'

MOTHER Lady day, Lady day. The men will return from the Labrador and dig some new potatoes. First potatoes of the year. Am I right, or, or …?

SON Lady bug, Lady bug. Fly away home, your house is on fire, your children are alone. *(Wanders off stage)*

MOTHER And Halloween. Halloween. We never had that. It was known as Colcannon night. Or Snap Apple night. What was the Colcannon? Well, it was a seven-vegetable dish served up as the main meal of the day. All the vegetables boiled up in the one pot. And Snap Apple … we'd hang apples from a beam and the youngsters would jump up trying to get an apple in their mouth. No trick-or-treating. No, that came in with the Americans in 1941. We'd duck for apples too. In the night, after supper and books. *(Lies back exhausted)* The mummering on Old Christmas Day. Not on Christmas Day. Not on Sundays. Feature how that would look. Could you just feature it now? Oh. Oh. *(Still exhausted, whispers last line)* Stop a nosebleed with a secret prayer. *(Lights fade)*

SON *(On kitchen side of stage)* Have to get that wood chopped up or laid out to dry against the back fence. Arthritis in my little finger. In my knee. Must ask Mother where her arthritis went to. She never complains about it anymore. Maybe old age wipes it out. Maybe she forgot she had it.

SON *(Wandering back to bedroom side of stage)* Mother, you don't complain about the arthritis anymore. What happened to that? *(Lights up on Mother)*

MOTHER What arthritis? I never had the arthritis. Next you'll be saying I had cancer. There was never any cancer in this family. Thank God. Same thing with TB. Your father never had the TB that time, it was some kind of rare German lung disease. He only had it in the one lung and everyone said it was TB. God-blessed fools. Simpletons, always pick the answer to everything off the plate of easy answers. He never had the TB. He got a tablet. A great big white pill like and he had to split that up four ways in order to take it down. The doctor had it flown in from Boston.

SON What? The pill? Had the pill flown in? Did it come cargo or have its own seat?

MOTHER What?

SON On account of the size you said.

MOTHER Oh, for God's sake, will you be quiet for a spell and let me think? All his family passed away young from TB. But not your father.

SON I'm going out to cut up that wood the Williams fellow brought. Mother, I got arthritis in my little finger.

MOTHER Chop it off.

SON What?

MOTHER You heard me. It's useless anyhow, the little finger.

SON Jesus, I think that's the little toe, girl. Through the evolutionary process the little toe has become redundant.

MOTHER What happened to my arthritis? I used to be filled up with it. Chock full. Now, not a stir of it.

SON Are you complaining? You never would have knowed if I hadn't mentioned it. Jesus, I'm glad you never got at my pinkie when I was young, Jesus. (*Sizes up his pinkie with love*) Have to get that wood chopped up or laid out to dry against the back fence now. (*Exits*)

MOTHER Mind the wind, mind the water rising. That time of the tidal wave, a woman went from window to window with a lighted candle in her hand as her house floated out the bay. They rescued her in St. Lawrence. Who'll be there to rescue you? Who'll be there to ferry you home?

Passage of time. Mother is asleep under a pile of blankets. Lights fade off from her. Up on Son as he re-enters with another armload of wood. He puts the kettle on. Makes tea, boils an egg, butters the toast and brings it all to the bedroom. Lights up on bedroom.

SON Got your tea here now. Your lunch, I suppose you'd call it.

MOTHER It's daytime. You wouldn't call it a lunch. A lunch is right before you goes to bed. That's my tea. What is it?

SON You're quite welcome, madam. No trouble really, no trouble at all. That Williams fellow what brought the wood, he was asking after you. Said he believes you're related to him somewheres off.

MOTHER Williams fellow? What Williams?

SON From out Isle Valen way, he said. On his mother's side, the Mulrooneys.

MOTHER The Mulrooneys? On his mother's side? A Williams? All the Mulrooneys that I ever knowed never got caught up with any Williamses. And all the Mulrooney girls were shipped out after their father died of the TB. Shockin' waste of a man, sober provider and knew his genealogy too. There was never any Williamses out in the bay, that's a town name. Or what came in with the Yanks.

SON I'm only telling you what he toldt to me. I'm only saying.

MOTHER He still out there? Go ask him what in the hell Mulrooney woman he's talking about.

SON He's gone. More wood to deliver. He wasn't here for the genealogy, he only mentioned it.

MOTHER Maybe it was Paddy Mulrooney … I dunno. See, Paddy wasn't really a Mulrooney. They took him and reared him, but he had youngsters and they were reared Mulrooneys on account of he took the name, see.

SON He looks like the Mulrooneys though, come to think of it. He really do, this young fellow. Like he got a strain of Mulrooney in him.

MOTHER A strain? There wasn't much watering down with the Mulrooneys, I'll tell you that.

SON In-bred, were they?

MOTHER Mind your tongue! In-bred indeed. Well … the hell's flames with them, why am I trying to pick up for them? Jesus, what did ole Bride Mulrooney ever do for me except help bring me into the world. Someone had to grab me and haul me out, or haul me in, whichever what way it was. Could have been anyone, really.

SON Ange is on her way out from town. Expect she'll be here soon now.

MOTHER You have anything on for her to eat? If she shows up.

SON Sure, she never eats anyway. Car full of chip bags and bar wrappers. And cigarette butts.

MOTHER I don't know what's the matter with her. Never marrying. No youngsters.

SON Got the good job though. That's something. Got the money in the bank.

MOTHER Most unhappy Christian I ever met, your sister. Always going around in circles. And all the questions like, "What was I like when I was two, Mother?" And "Was I any good in school, Mother?" Always looking for answers, answers, answers. Don't even realize that the greatest pull lies in the question itself. How much does a loaf of bread cost? Easy. How much of your soul did it cost to earn the bread? Question.

SON Good one, Mudder. Sometimes you amazes me. What comes out of you. Eat that egg now before it goes cold. It's not hard-boiled or anything. And your tea is strong and hot. Drink it now.

MOTHER That Williams fellow? Any red in his hair? Or fair-skinned?

SON Black as coal. Fair-skinned though. The black Irish. Freckles like fallen stars.

MOTHER Freckles. Old Paddy had them when he was young. I wonder now … if on his mother's side …

SON You got to eat more. Ange'll accuse me of trying to starve you. She'll have you packed off to the home if you don't make an attempt at showin' her you're able to take care of yourself. Or at least eat for yourself.

MOTHER I'm not packing off to anywhere, except the final stop. Why is she concerned about me now? She never was before. What bee do she have in her bonnet about me now for?

SON That's two questions.

MOTHER What?

SON Two questions. Number one: What bee do she have in her bonnet? And, number two: Why is she concerned about me now for?

MOTHER That's one.

SON Two, I think. The bee, and why now?

MOTHER Get me my comb, will you? I'll draw it across my scalp so she don't go staring hard at me. What about that bit of moose stew from yesterday? You could heat that up for us all.

SON She's not going to eat moose. She was talking about pasta or pastral, or some such, that last time she was here.

MOTHER That sounds like Latin. You can't eat Latin. Can't speak it either. Why, in the name of God, did they teach Latin to ye in school when they knew it wasn't used anymore? Trying to put ye to sleep in school and then ye'd come home all restless like. When ye should have been worn out from learnin'. I remember my grandfather had a book from Ireland, it was about the old teachers, scholars they were. The original teachers. They had a pack of knowledge, according to this book. After they died off it was only watered-down learning. It's all workers, no scholars. If it was a factory with a pension at the end of it, that'd be good enough. See? See what I mean?

SON *(Looks out the window)* There she is. There's Ange. You gonna get up and sit in the chair for her?

MOTHER No! Let her see me as I really am.

SON In that case, I'll just mosey on back to the wood.

MOTHER Just like your father to the tee. *(She sits there and stares straight ahead. Lights fade)*

SCENE FIVE
Lights up on kitchen, old woman sitting on bed, turned to wall, back to audience.

Ange enters with wind catching at the door. She hauls it through breathless. Mother is still in bed.

ANGE What a wind! I forget how the wind swoops down out here. It could knock you off your feet. Hello, Mother. How are you?

MOTHER Same. Same. No change in me. Only another day older and no deeper in debt, like Tennessee Ernie Ford used to say.

ANGE You're looking pretty good. *(Takes a chair to sit by the bed)* Real good. No change at all.

MOTHER That's what I toldt you. No change in me. Are you after putting on weight?

ANGE *(Flattening down her blouse against her pants)* No, I dunno. I think it's the material in this blouse. It won't lay down. Puffs up.

MOTHER Tommy is out back at the wood. He'll make us tea soon, if you're hungry.

ANGE No, Mother. I ate on the way out. I might grab a hamburger at Moorlands on my way back.

MOTHER Talking about turning around and going back and you just got here?

ANGE No, I'm only saying. I'm only saying. Did you get your hair cut since the last time I saw you?

MOTHER No. Oh, I chops at it with the scissors. But they're blunt. I have to saw at it, might as well use the bread knife. Do a better job.

ANGE Christ, Mother. I'll take you to the hairdresser. Just have Tommy make an appointment some day you know I'm coming out. I'll take you. Don't be sawing at your hair.

MOTHER It's no odds, Angela. What difference does it make. No one comes in, only the priest and he's not after a woman. Or Mrs. Moriarity with the blessed sacrament on Saturdays and she's as blind as meself. I don't need any hairdresser.

ANGE You always used to go to the hairdresser. I was reading in a magazine that older people shouldn't let themselves go or depression could set in.

MOTHER Older people ... well, I'm old. I expects you goes to a hairdresser.

ANGE Well, yes. I do have to keep up appearances for my work and all.

MOTHER You mean that if it wasn't for your work, you wouldn't keep up appearances. That sounds depressed to me.

ANGE Well, I'm not depressed, sorry to have to report. I'm doing just fine.

MOTHER Either sign of a boyfriend or what?

ANGE *(Laughs)* No ... neither sign, hide nor hair. Not that I go looking. And I suppose neither one is going to come looking for me either. Now that I'm middle-age.

MOTHER You're not old. Why is it that Patsy was the only one of ye to settle down?

ANGE Well, I'd say that Tommy is pretty settled down now, isn't he?

MOTHER Poor Tommy. He's not well. No girl would want Tommy.

ANGE Tommy is so well. What's wrong with Tommy? Nothing. It's that he feels obliged ... like.

MOTHER Obliged? Obliged to do what? To take care of me? Is that what you're saying? Well, Tommy is not taking care of me. I'm taking care of him. In case you never noticed, it's my pension that pays the bills around here.

ANGE I guess you're taking care of one another then. Kinda like co-dependent or something.

MOTHER He said you wanted me to go into the home.

ANGE What! I never. I never. I might have suggested that ye investigate the formalities, so ye'd know when, if, ye needed to.

MOTHER When. If. The formalities. Jesus, Mary and Christ. I'm not going nowhere. This is my home. He needs me. How would he live?

ANGE He could get a job, Mother.

MOTHER A job? Where? He'd have to go away. He'd be miserable. And I'd be miserable in the home. The home. Why do they call it that? It's no more a home than it is a boiled boot.

ANGE Maybe you only thinks he wouldn't be able to get along. And maybe you only think you wouldn't like it there.

MOTHER Maybe. Maybe. Maybe. Why is it that you're so concerned about me now? So what is it about me staying in my own home that bothers you so much? Tell me that.

ANGE I'm just worried, is all. It might be hard on Tommy and it might get harder. You got no one to wash you, Mother.

MOTHER I can wash myself! I can give myself a sponge bath any day of the week. Your father took a bath once a year. Easter Saturday night. And he never smelled bad.

ANGE Dad took one bath a year! You've got to be kidding! You never told me that before.

MOTHER And why should I? It's not exactly dinner conversation.

ANGE Dad always smelled great. I mean, it was his smell. Like wood smoke and tar. Kinda musky. My God, once a year!

MOTHER You never asks nothing about your line. About your family. There's cousins of yours living in town and you wouldn't know them if you bumped into them down to Woolworth's.

ANGE There's no more Woolworth's. I doubt I'd have anything in common with cousins, Mother.

MOTHER What's that got to do with it? You're breaking the line by not visiting your cousins. We always stayed with relatives when we took the train into town. Whether we knew them or not. Sure, we got to know them. You took them in a load of homemade bread, some dried capelin, bit of salt fish, bit of moose, tub of berries. We were right grateful to have a cup of tea in a place that wasn't a restaurant. Nowadays ye'd rather eat in a restaurant amongst strangers.

ANGE Yeah, I would actually.

MOTHER Another sign of depression, I'd say.

Ange sits, still looking depressed.

ANGE Do you hear from Patsy?

MOTHER Yes, girl, regularly! I always dreads the end of our talks. She always signs off saying, "The Lord be with you." The Lord be with you? She's a Catholic. Catholics don't talk like that. Maybe God bless you now, or something. Or, God love you, my love. Patsy is still a Catholic even if she did change her religion. She's a Catholic and that's that. For Christ's sake.

ANGE You can't force someone into being what they don't want to be.

MOTHER Force has nothing to do with it. It's like blood, for God's sake. A Catholic is a Catholic.

ANGE Unless you're excommunicated.

MOTHER No one in this family would ever, ever, ever, be let out of the Catholic church. Patsy is still a Catholic like a black is a black. And that's that.

ANGE Mother? Mother, was I good at anything when I was young?

MOTHER What?

ANGE Was I good at anything? When I was small.

MOTHER There you go again. How am I supposed to remember. I reared four of ye. Ye all blends together.

ANGE Nothing stands out? Didn't I ever say anything cute, like?

MOTHER Cute? That's an American word. Like cookie and divorce. They were never in our vocabulary till the Yanks came here. We'd say nice-looking and biscuit. And there was never any divorce.

ANGE *(Sighs)* Where's Tommy, did you say? I'll go say hello.

MOTHER He's out back piling wood, I suppose. Tell him you wants your tea and to put on the moose with it.

Ange exits.

SCENE SIX
Lights up on Mother.

MOTHER And what trade, says he to him, have you? Oh he knows nothing. How could he? He never left the corner of the hearth. He grew up stooped and numb as if he was too long in too strong a wind. *(Pauses)* It's quiet now. Always quiet after someone is here. And after someone has been gone a long time it gets noisy with the voices humming in my head. Is she my daughter? She seems foreign. Like a visitor. When she was small I knew her. I took her around. Kept her clean. Put her in school. Took her to mass. What was she asking? When she was young? Oh, the wake. I should have toldt her that. See if she remembers ole Mrs. Corrigan. That was the last wake in the place. And it was fitting it be for Anastasia. I picked young Ange up and held her over Anastasia to kiss her cheek. And Ange kicked at me … kicked me in the shins and I dropped her on top of poor Ansty in the casket. Oh my Christ, Ange howled like a cat stuck into her, like she was a cat in a cat fight. I expect she never got over it really. Oh my. I'll take a little nap now and tell her when I wakes up. She's always asking. I'll sleep with my socks on so they can't take them off me. The fairies are cuteness itself, but I'm able for them.

SCENE SEVEN
Lights fade on bedroom and up on kitchen. Ange and Tommy come in, both bearing wood.

SON You should have put on the ole lumber jacket to keep the turpentine off you.

ANGE Na, I don't like this blouse anyway. Don't know why I bought it.

SON Sure, it's nice. Lively colour. Suits you.

ANGE *(Delighted)* Thanks. I'll put the kettle on.

SON There's cake there. Jellyroll or lemon sodas or some such thing.

ANGE Biscuits, not cookies. Nice-looking, not cute. No divorce.

SON What?

ANGE Oh, just Mother. With her old ways, the words really mean a lot to her, don't they?

SON You should hear her litany sometimes. She goes over everything as if she was a shopkeeper taking stock.

ANGE Do you ever worry that you're getting like her?

SON Like her? No. Why?

ANGE It's like ye have a secret language or something sometimes.

SON We're just used to one another is all.

ANGE I don't know if that's healthy, Tommy.

SON Healthy? Well, I don't know about that. But, you know, Ange, speaking on health, it seems to me that you don't eat all that well. I mean it's none of my business, I suppose, but you only picks here, and then there's chip bags and bar wrappers all over your car every time I'm in it. I mean, I'm only saying …

ANGE *(Upset)* So, you're only saying that I'm probably physically unhealthy and I'm only saying that you're probably mentally unhealthy. And I'm only saying that probably Mother is a bit of both and on the way to more of the same. Can I clean here, would you mind?

SON Knock yourself out, only leave this area alone. *(Points to wood pile)* I have them stacked just so.

ANGE Do you ever worry, Tommy, that you might become more alienated?

SON From what?

ANGE The world.

SON The world is right here. Or as much of it as can fit here.

ANGE Mother toldt me you said I said she should go into the home.

SON Well, didn't you?

ANGE Not in so many words. I might have thought out loud to you, or put forth the idea like.

SON So which is it?

ANGE Well, if she was in the home, you would be able to work.

SON Oh yeah. Where? The fishery? An automobile plant? The high rise up the lane? The smelter?

ANGE You could move.

SON Oh, just like that. Even if I didn't want to.

ANGE Well, for work.

SON No, I'm Catholic.

ANGE What's that got to do with it?

SON Maybe I can't move because this is in my blood, like being a Catholic.

ANGE God, you're just like her. And you've given up.

SON Given in … to myself.

ANGE You encourage her dementia.

SON I understand it.

ANGE Jesus, did it ever hit you that you could be losing it along with her?

SON There might be more to it, Ange, than nonsense. Ever think of that?

ANGE Oh, like tradition, knowledge, all that elder shit. We're not native, Tommy, ever notice that?

SON What? You got to be native to have elders, parents, a way of life?

ANGE Next thing, you'll be getting a grant to study her or something. To preserve her way of talking. It's all shit and you know it. What are you, a folklorist now?

SON *(Emphasizes)* I'm her son. *(Lights fade)*

SCENE EIGHT
Lights up on Mother in bed. She is continuing a story that the audience comes in on.

MOTHER And so, the old fellow, he says to Pakey, "Pakey," he says, "Pakey b'y, it's all about a great injustice that was done to me."

MOTHER Who are you? Where did you come from? I toldt you not to come snooping around here anymore. Goddamn you to hell's flames!

ANGE Mother, it's me.

MOTHER Me, me, me! That's all it was ever about, wasn't it? And now you're back to plague me. What? You never had the time of day for me before and now every time I opens my eyes you're there smirking at me. Just go to Christ out of it. *(Turns to wall)*

ANGE *(Starts to cry)* Mother, please stop it. I just can't take it, Mother. I need you. *(Laughs)* Oops! Forget that, if you remember it.

MOTHER Where's Tommy with me tea? Who are you?

ANGE I could be the tea server, if you want. That'd be easy. *(Exits)*

MOTHER Tommy! Tommy!

Tommy and Ange meet in middle of stage. They pass each other like strangers on a street. Ange goes to kitchen. Tommy goes to the bedroom.

SON I'm here! Have no fear … number one son to the rescue!

MOTHER Had that visitor again?

SON Which half?

MOTHER The whole kit and kaboodle this time. And she going on about herself. And laughing at me.

SON A woman this time. She's more frequent now. Tryin' to take over, is she?

MOTHER Yes! Mind! Why she's here is beyond me. Well, she won't get past me. She won't get over my time. No, by the Christ! Where's my tea to, Tommy? Are you late or am I all turned around?

SON You're coming over to the table now. Do you remember that Ange is here? She's making a tea for us.

MOTHER Ange? Here? When did she get here? While I was asleep? Was I asleep?

SON *(Lifts her up and puts her slippers on)* Come on now and Ange will tell you all about it.

They take a long time to cross the stage to the kitchen. Ange is setting the table and stirring the pot on stove. She seems shy and shaken.

MOTHER When did you get here? What's that you're making?

ANGE It's the moose stew like Tommy said you wanted.

MOTHER Ye have that. I'll have my tea and a bit of biscuit or something.

SON There's plenty, Mother. You need to eat the meat for protein. Stop filling up on biscuits. Only fog. You're worse than Ange here.

ANGE I eats ... mostly in restaurants.

MOTHER Like to have your money. Speaking of restaurants, I dreamt that Woolworth's was gone off Water Street. Sure, that can't be.

ANGE *(Sighs)* Been gone for years, Mother.

MOTHER What's there now?

ANGE Nothing. Empty building. Nothing.

MOTHER Nothing! Can't someone tell that useless mayor to get off his fat arse. Why do ye put up with it?

ANGE Oh, it's our fault, is it, that there's nothing where Woolworth's was? That's choice. That's one I'm not touching.

MOTHER What? I'm not asking you to touch it. Just do something about it. You sells buildings, don't you?

ANGE Mother, can we talk about something else, please?

MOTHER Why are you using the good china? That's for the priest, or relatives from away. Where's my mug?

Tommy replaces china with mug. Ange replaces mug with china. Tommy replaces china with mug.

ANGE Why not use it, Mother? It's only sitting there collecting dust. It's very elegant.

MOTHER And if the priest comes and it's broke? Then what? Nothing. You don't know nothing about saving things. About there being a time and place for everything. You'd swear I never raised you. That you were drug up. Kept in the yard on a clothesline or something.

SON I think Ange only wants you to have a nice cup and saucer to drink out of. She only served it to you. You and you alone.

MOTHER Well, I don't want it. Put it back.

ANGE Put it back yourself.

MOTHER What?

ANGE You heard me. Put it back yourself if you're so fussy and if you're so healthy that you can walk over there and do it. Go on. *(Lights sharply out)*

SCENE NINE

Lights up on bedroom. Tommy is fluffing up pillow. Mother is on her knees by bed saying the rosary. She crosses herself and gets up. Tommy helps her into the bed.

SON I'll bring you in that radio that's repaired so you can listen to a bit of music now.

MOTHER Yes, that'd be nice. Smooth the savage beast that must be me.

SON Never mind now. Don't bother yourself. Comfy?

MOTHER Did you see the way she turned on me? Right out of the blue. Must have been brewing for some long spell.

SON The priest'll be in this evening now. He'll hear your confession. And then Mrs. Moriarity with the host. That'll help you relax.

MOTHER I'm relaxed. Why wouldn't I be? Take more than her to upset me. All I've been through in my lifetime. That was nothing. It's her problem, not mine. Her a grown woman, acting like a child. That's the Moriarity blood in her. I always knew it would show itself sooner or later. All the Moriaritys were either mental or alcoholics.

SON Didn't Albert Moriarity marry an O'Flaherty from up the line and that one's father used to get up on the bridge and howl at the moon when it was full?

MOTHER An O'Flaherty? Who, Albert? No, b'y. And that's what he did not. Those O'Flahertys never married outside the area and there's your problem. They said he used to froth at the mouth and everything. Nicest kind of a man the rest of the time. But it would come over him and that'd be that.

SON What about those two brothers up there, who are in that whatchama-call-it home? Weren't they tangled up with that family somehow?

MOTHER What two brothers, b'y? I can't read your mind.

SON The two that were found left in that house up Notre Dame Bay way. They couldn't talk and wherever one would go, the other would be right behind. They couldn't be separated at all. One was like the shadow of the other. They'd have to sleep in the same bed and everything. No more than three feet between them ever.

MOTHER Poor souls. But sure, how could they be connected to the O'Flahertys? All the area is the one line, more or less. Two lines, I suppose, Moriaritys and O'Flahertys.

SON That's why I figured the brothers were connected, on account of the way they are. Is it true that there's more fairies in this area than there is anywhere else?

MOTHER The fairies is everywhere. More in Ireland I'd expect than anywhere else. The Protestants can't see them, that's what I heard tell.

SON And don't you mind them? I mean, don't you fear them like?

MOTHER Well, you'd fear them till you got used to them. If you're reared with them, you learns to respect them. Give them a wide berth. The fairies can't help who they are on account of being the fallen angels. Is there any more of them lemon biscuits there?

SON Yes, but you're not getting them. You'll spoil your lunch tonight. What about that woman who was afraid of cars?

MOTHER Poor Mrs. Laura that was. Poor soul.

SON What was her problem?

MOTHER Problem? What makes you think she had a problem? Since when is being afraid of cars a problem?

SON Well, I mean what's to be afraid of?

MOTHER If you were reared on an island in the bay and you never saw a piece of machinery in your life, let alone a car, you can't tell me you'd be relaxed like, if one drove up behind you.

SON We used to come behind her and go "beep, beep."

MOTHER That's a sin for you. If I had a heard tell of that, you'd be banished, I tell you.

SON She used to throw out transistor radios too, after the batteries died.

MOTHER That's where them load of small radios came from. Poor soul, her. She was from Red Island, strange crew some of them Reds were. They could be traced back to Cork, almost the whole island. They say the Cork people were a very clickish bunch on account of it being a strong rebel area. Michael Collins and all.

SON When are you talking about, Mother?

MOTHER When? When what?

SON Michael Collins fellow.

MOTHER Early part of the 1900s, I suppose. Out in the bay people kept up on what was going on over the water. When Michael Collins was kilt, Red Island went nuts. The men were drunk for a week. The women, to this day, well my day, curses Michael Collins, and I expect I'm the only one left knows why. Are you going to bring me that bickie now, or what?

SON No, I toldt you. You'll spoil your lunch. Now tell me … about Father working for the Norwegians. Tell me about that before you has your nap. And then you'll get your lunch after you has your nap. Where did Father go out from?

MOTHER With the Norwegians? Out of Rose au Rue. Just like the song: "Out of Rose au Rue we sailed to hunt the big fish down." Where do Pat and Joe Byrne be to now? They were some singers. Oh my, they come from Great Paradise too, the same place the Mulrooneys come from. Lovely looking men too. Patsy used to beat around with one of them, I can't remember, the big fellow, I think it was. Great strong timbre of a voice on him. Lovely manners too. Old Paradise manners, the like you don't see in the town. All them men, their fathers great big blocks of men, they were. All the men now are scrawny as scarecrows. No health to them. Who'd want a scrawny man around the house, not able to lift his hand to anything.

SON Father was thin.

MOTHER Your father wasn't well all his life. That German disease. It stripped him. But he was a hard worker, despite that.

SON The Norwegians, Mother, get to Rose au Rue.

MOTHER Big rusted factory there now. Remains of the whaling station. I come into Rose au Rue one time on Warehams' boat, the *Berta Joyce*. We were going into Meersheen for something or other and oh my … did I ever tell you about the man who used to wear skirts and dresses? Oh my, big strap of a fellow but ever since he was small, his mother donned him in dresses so the fairies

wouldn't snatch him cause he was her only boy, see.
And he liked it. Liked the skirts and such. He was on the
wharf that day we were pulling in, oh, so Wareham
could pick up a load of fish, sure. And, now I can't get his
name to me, but he was sitting on the wharf as we were
tacking in and the hills were blocked with fog, and the
stillness, oh my … was breathless. And sitting there was
the remains of the old whaling station like great hulks of
whales themselves, they were, and shimmering out of the
fog was ole, oh my yes! Old Gussie Flynn was his name.
Shimmering out of the fog with his legs dangling over
the wharf and his knees showing white. Lovely dress he
had on him too. Garden party dress, you know, that
Dan River material with the puckers. He looked
gorgeous, really.

SON And no one thought it queer? I mean strange, that
he'd be wearing dresses sitting on a wharf, or sitting
anywhere, I s'pose?

MOTHER Sure, it wasn't queer. It was normal, I'm
telling you. It'd be queer not to if you was raised that
way.

SON Funny ole world, isn't it? But what about Father
going up to Hawke Harbour on the Labrador. Tell me
about that now.

MOTHER Only man I ever met with no fun in him.
You'd think he was a Protestant. Never drank, had the
same bottle of Haig ale from one Christmas to the
next. Made a rubber stopper for it, so it wouldn't go flat.
Never danced, and me the best dancer, so they say, I'm
only saying. I had sixty-three steps. Only ole Mart
Canning had more … sixty-five. He said he had made
them up after he saw me having sixty-three over on
Meersheen. Some competition in that man, tis no wonder
he had all boys, eleven of them. Did you know that if you
wants to have a boy, eat salt, and if you wants to have a

girl, eat cream? I'm telling you. You getting' all this? You gettin' all this, Tommy. I'm very tired.

SON Nap now. Nap now, Mother, I'm going to make sure the stove don't go low. The fire don't go low. I'll bring in your tea bom by.

Tommy exits and enters in the kitchen.

SCENE TEN
Lights down on Mother. Kitchen door opens. Ange stands there. Son looks up.

SON Jesus! I'd thought you'd be back on Cochrane Street by now. Come in, come in, you're heating the harbour.

ANGE I never went back. I went up to Shaw's Lane and looked out over the arm. Thinking.

SON And how far did that get you?

ANGE All the way back here. I can never get far from here anyway. *(Unbuttons her coat, hangs it up and puts the kettle on)* Something I don't understand. I'm screwed up.

SON Join the clan. Sure, Ange, surely you've noticed by now that there's no one in our line what isn't. You takes it too hard.

ANGE Father wasn't screwed up.

SON Only the most solitary man on the face of the Earth, other than Jesus in the dessert. And He came out of the dessert.

ANGE That's not screwed up. Just different. But you can't say Mother hasn't always been really friggin' nuts, but functional, Tommy. I mean I'm not talking about the dementia. I mean always. I mean look at us. Too screwed up to have a full-blown adult relationship.

SON Patsy is in the family. She's married.

ANGE Yeah, to Mr. Redneck-Arsehole-Baptist-Screamer-Preacher. Has to sneak her daily dose of gin and sneak calls to the "Newfs" back home. Has to wash his feet. Healthy. Healthy. Healthy. He's a friggin' dose. Her life sucks and you know it.

SON Yeah, but it's her life. You need to step back maybe, Ange. Reconsider things.

ANGE Plant a garden, like you, so that I can chill out. I can't. She drives me, Tommy. She knows how to get under my skin big time. Every friggin' time. I just can't escape her.

SON Well, you do live in St. John's, Ange.

ANGE So what are you saying? That I should be out more. Be more involved?

SON No, I'm not saying that. I'm saying that you have lots of opportunity to have your own life without Mother getting to you.

ANGE She'd get to me anywhere, Tommy, for Christ's sake. It's like she … she bored her way in under my skin and is lodged there permanently. No matter where I go.

SON I think that's called family.

ANGE Isn't the idea of family supposed to be support and love.

SON She loves you, Ange, in her fashion.

ANGE In her fashion! In her fashion! Lord Christ. In her own way, in her own time.

SON This isn't *Father Knows Best*, Ange. Or some Hollywood fifties family. It is what it is, so why not try and live within it?

ANGE Jesus, Tommy. You're so friggin' stoic that you're almost catatonic. Is there no fight in you at all?

SON I'll save my fight for the real enemy. Ange, did it ever dawn on you that you aren't a kid anymore?

ANGE I was never a kid, Tommy. She used me to be her … her … I don't know what. She saw my weakness and she used it. She saw me watching her and sucked me in. Why can't you admit growing up in this house meant moving around her and her insanity. But she was cute because she was never nuts to the outside world, and so she got away with it. What's that old expression … "angel on the road, devil at home."

SON She had a hard life growing up. And then her and Dad were like chalk and cheese.

ANGE And we paid for her miserable life. A total narcissistic personality. In love with her own misery.

SON I wouldn't say that. She hated her life, and if there was any problem it was that hate.

ANGE Okay, I can accept that. But why did we have to suffer?

SON Well, there wasn't access to shrinks back then. There was only the priests and they weren't exactly unbiased.

ANGE Did you grow up in the same house? Jesus.

SON You know I've had my battles, Ange. The booze, the pills. The works. A family burger with the works, that's us. A bay-whopper. But she's old now, and I'm just trying to go with the flow. And there are moments, good ones. She's got a great sense of humour, you know.

ANGE No. I don't. I just can't seem to disassociate like you can. And I can't get interested it all that genealogy and folklore crap.

SON It's stories, Ange. It's like turning on the television and there's a schooner ran aground or a great big sea heaving up somewhere. It's all the stuff she has stored and she wants it out.

ANGE Yeah, well, any family gemstones there? Any stories of killing the family dog or leaving your child outdoors overnight to teach her a lesson in coming home on time?

SON She goes over that when she thinks I'm not listening. She is plagued too, Ange.

ANGE Good. *(Lights fade)*

SCENE ELEVEN
Lights up on Ange on the daybed with the lumber jacket over her shoulders. Tommy is putting wood in the fire. Ange stirs and wakes up.

ANGE What? Did I fall asleep? How did I fall asleep? The last I remember …

SON You, ah, had a bit of a crying spell. Ange, did you have a drop to drink up there in Shaw's Lane? A flask in the glove compartment?

ANGE *(Fixes herself)* Ah, Christ, I feel like shit. What time is it, Tommy? Is it dark?

SON It is. It's six o'clock. I'll have to be waking herself now, or else she'll be up all night.

ANGE No, don't. Wait. Wait till I'm gone. I can't go another round with her in one day.

SON Up to yourself. Better scatter then. She's usually on deck sooner than this.

ANGE *(Gathers her purse)* Okay and … call me, you know, if there's anything.

Ange exits.

SON *(To himself)* Yeah, right. If there's anything. *(Goes towards the bedroom side of the stage)* Like she remembers what you did when you were three-and-a-half on June the 24th at 3:15 p.m. Righto. *(Enters bedroom)* Oyez! Oyez! Calling on the queen of this establishment. Are ye of sound-ish mind and able-ish body? Can ye hear me at all?

Mother stirs slowly. Starts talking from under the pile of blankets.

MOTHER *(Digs around under the blankets and hauls up a long wool sock with a rock in the end of it)* The rock is after going cold. Stone-cold the rock is.

SON Rock as cold as a stone. What's the difference betwixt a stone and a rock, Mother?

MOTHER What? Are you at it again? Trying to confuse me. What time of the day or night is it?

SON It's late now. You're after sleeping odd. Your naps are usually over by four o'clock and now it's past six.

MOTHER Six? In the morning? It can't be night.

SON Evening. Evening, I'd say. But then again I wouldn't say night till late evening. More after tenish you'd say night, right?

MOTHER What have you been at? *(Throws arm out towards the kitchen)* Drawing wisdom from the fire, is that it? Wasting your time and wasting wood by keeping the fire up. There's no need to be keeping the wood to that fire until you has to cook a meal. Too much waste goes on in this house. Where's your father?

SON Ah, *(Stumped)* dead.

MOTHER *(Leans in close to size him up)* You're cute. Or thinks you are. Have you anything for me to eat?

SON You know, Mother, you're too much for one mind to ponder. You really are. Ange just left.

MOTHER All babies cry their first view of the sea.

SON What has that got to do with the price of tea in Russia?

MOTHER China! Ha! Thinks you're cute, is all. Only thinks it.

SON I don't even think it, Mudder, and that's more to pity, isn't it? Truth be known, Mother, I'm feeling kinda blue. Depressed like.

MOTHER What? You? What in the name of God do you have to be depressed about? Oh, spare me, please. *(Turns to the wall)*

SON That's all we've ever been doing in this house, Mother, is sparing you. At the cost of our own peace of mind. *(Lights fade)*

SCENE TWELVE

Lights up on kitchen. The door opens off the kitchen. Son gets up and goes to kitchen part of stage. Ange is standing there, car keys in her hand.

ANGE Car is dead. Not a gig in her. Dead as a dick.

SON Don't go saying that around, Mother. She'll say you're only trying to confuse her.

ANGE So, she's still kickin? Still spoutin' her pearls of wisdom?

SON She just asked me where Father was. What happened to the car?

ANGE Your guess is probably better than mine. Just dead. D-E-D. And I think I shouldn't drive anyway. I did drink a flask at Shaw's Lane. I'll fess up.

SON *(Pulls on his belt buckle western style and talks like a cowboy)* Well, hunker down then. I'll put the kettle on and rustle up some chow.

ANGE How is she? Resting peacefully, as they say?

SON Yeah, she was muttering something about babies having their first view of the sea. That was after I told her that you had just left.

ANGE *(Startled)* Babies what? Babies all cry their first view of the sea? I remember that. I remember her saying that to me. Christ, I can't believe that. I actually have a memory. Did she say she said it to me?

SON Yeah, I think. Yeah, she did. After I mentioned your name, she said it.

ANGE I don't want to drive back. I think I should stay the night like. I mean, if it's all right.

SON Don't see why not. I mean, it could mean another meal together. A tea and toast type, at the very least.

ANGE I could sleep on the davenport if it still pulls out.

SON I don't think it's called a davenport anymore.

ANGE Chesterfield?

SON Couch?

ANGE Sofa?

SON Daybed.

ANGE Oh, Christ. But remember when Dad would heave off on the daybed after Sunday dinner. Like every man in every bay and every cove, like clockwork in every kitchen in outport Newfoundland.

SCENE THIRTEEN
Lights up on kitchen, Ange and Son. Old woman in the dark, sitting on bed, turned to wall, back to audience.

ANGE Okay. So is she aware I'm here? No. So, I'll go in. *(Uses her hands to flatten down her blouse and sits down on kitchen chair, hesitates. Lights stay on her a long time as she sits in the chair.)*

SON She's holding court and you can be next in line.

ANGE Here goes nothing.

SON She don't bite. Or at least not with her false teeth out.

Son exits.

ANGE Comforting thought. Okay then, here I go.

MOTHER What, yes mind! Get out of that and leave that stuff alone.

ANGE Mother ... Mom, are you all right?

MOTHER *(Looks at her after taking her eyes away from the shelf near the ceiling)* Tell that crowd to leave that alone. That's mine. You got to watch them every minute of the day. And they're sly. Cute as dolls.

ANGE Mother, there's no one there. There's no one at your stuff.

MOTHER What? No one at my stuff? Then where is it all getting to. I'm robbed blind I tell you.

ANGE Mother, there's no one to take your stuff. Who would take your stuff? The fairies?

MOTHER *(Looks at her mistrustfully)* The fairies? Since when did you start believing in them? The fairies. Mind. It's that crowd Tommy has in is taking it. Fairies don't go after clothes, except the socks. Everyone knows that.

ANGE Oh. Everyone. And why do the fairies just want socks?

MOTHER How, in the name of God, do I know that? Anyway, they don't want the socks. They only wants to addle you. That's their life. It got nothing to do with want. Am I getting something to eat this day?

MOTHER Whist. Whist. You hear that? Goddamned things. Trying to trip me up. Trying to get the better of me. Where are my socks? And my good dresses? Where are they?

ANGE Your socks are here … somewhere I'm sure, Mother. *(Starts to search frantically, getting on her knees and looking under her mother's bed.)*

MOTHER And my dresses? How do you know where anything is? You don't know anything about this place. You're never here.

ANGE I'm here. I'm here now. I'm here often enough. You don't ever seem glad I'm here anyhow, so what odds is it, my being here? *(There is panic in her voice.)*

MOTHER Odds? Odds? Where is my stuff I'm telling you. Are you after giving it away? Or taking it? What do you want with my things? All the money you're making. Someone's after taking from me everything I'm the owned of.

ANGE For God's sake, Mother, I'm not touching your stuff! Stop accusing me. Stop talking to me like that. I'm trying to help you. *(Starts looking around the room for the "stuff")*

MOTHER And lock the door, lock the door! Tommy thinks nobody's ever going to come in here and steal my money, but I knows better … I knows.

ANGE Don't worry, Mother. I'll close up the house for the night. I won't forget. *(Goes to the curtain)*

MOTHER Mind you don't forget and don't you forget that the Williamses was never related to the Mulrooneys.

ANGE *(At curtain)* I'm closing it up … I'll batten down the hatches and yes, Mother, the Williamses were never related to the Mulrooneys.

MOTHER And the Moriaritys, they were from, from …

ANGE From Garden Cove.

MOTHER From where? What? How do you know that?

ANGE I know, Mother, because you told me ... I know.

SOLO THE PEDDLER

Approximately 50 minutes

Solo the Peddler has not yet been produced.

Written in 2009 but not yet produced by Tramore, *Solo the Peddler* tells the story of a Lebanese peddler who walked the Cape Shore of Placentia Bay with a two-hundred pound pack on his back. His wares often came from shipwrecks off the coast. He was one of many peddlers who had their regions all over the island. Joseph Solo (Sulieman Yousif Saleh) eventually married a local girl and made the Cape Shore his home. The play tells of his life in the old country and his rather unorthodox marriage on the Cape Shore. The play is a tale of the triumph of the soul over hardship and adversity. This play contains fictional elements based on oral history.

LIST OF CHARACTERS

SOLO
KITTY BOWE
NANCY
MR. FOLEY
MAN IN COMMUNITY

Music is playing off stage. A long haunting drone of Eastern pipes followed by a voice lamenting in Arabic. Solo enters. He walks across the stage with a large peddler's pack on his back. He is singing the song, the lament. He ends the song, takes off his pack and sits on it. From his pocket he pulls an orange and tosses it into the air and catches it.

SOLO An orange. Imagine! A fruit from the sun. *(He peels it slowly, humming and singing in his language. Each section he peels he holds up and comments on.)* Here is Majdal Sharm in 1888. My village. A village filled with the sun. Filled with light. Filled with oranges. Filled with … problems. *(Throws an orange section to the floor and looks at the audience)* My village … it is far away. *(Throws an arm into the air)* In my country … there are people everywhere. Muslims and Christians claw at each other for space because they think the other is wrong … about everything. Everything. There is blood everywhere. I told my father I must go. The French came in during my father's time, as peacekeepers and occupiers. They protected the Christians. But with the French, the area's old ways were destroyed. Our small shops closed. They could not compete against the cheap foreign goods. The franc replaced gold and our currency was debased.

SOLO Even in my father's time there was massive movement in southern and eastern Europe. America. *(Stands up and stretches one arm over his head)* The statue of liberty. So many have gone to the land of opportunity so that they could return home to start up a farm or a small business. Four months on the sea to travel to the new world. But there were already so many of us there. Lebanese everywhere. Some struck out for less greener pastures … Halifax, even St. John's, Newfoundland. *(Kicks at his backpack)* This is my best friend. This … is my bread. My burden. Forty-seven families here on the island now: Aheys, Altiens, Andrews, Basha, Boulas,

Corbage, Ellis, Faour, Gaultois, George, Gossine, Joseph, Kelly, Michael, Nickosey, Noah, Richard, Sapp, Simon, Sphire, Solo, Thomas, Tootan, Tuma. But I am a free man. I walk the roads, the birds sing to me, the sun shines on me ... sometimes, the fog shrouds me. I look to the sea and the fishermen are in their small boats. They are free too. Me on the land, them on the water. We are linked in a common bond, the peddler and the fisher.

SOLO And now my pack is full again. My good fortune of a full pack comes from the misfortune of others. Not that I caused any misfortune. No ... never! But the good ship, the *Marvale* struck off of Cape Freels Rock. Her holds were flooded. A good ship, so I'm told. Seven thousand net ton, built in 1907 in Glasgow. She was a troop ship originally built to carry soldiers in the First World War. Many Newfoundland soldiers returned home on this ship. But on her final voyage she was carrying two hundred passengers and a cargo of wheat and farm products. On the 21st of May in 1923, she was steaming through thick fog all day. The tides hauled her too near the land and at 4 p.m. she ran upon Cape Freels Rock, one and a half miles from the nearest land at Cape Pine. The captain was going to try to beach the ship. He managed to get all four hundred and sixty-three passengers and crew off the ship, and rowed into St. Shotts. St. Shotts has a population of about one hundred people. It had a limited supply of food and shelter for such a great influx of people. The captain walked to Trepassey, fourteen miles away. Early the next morning several ships steamed to St. Shotts to take the passengers to a larger centre. On May 23rd the captain went to St. John's to report on what could be salvaged from his ship. There was bacon, ham and cheese in the hold.

SOLO In June, the safes were removed from the purser's room. When the divers opened the holds, all the cargo

was gone. Some had been driven ashore, more to sea.
The ship was breaking up fast on the rugged reef in the
heavy seas. Some cargo was left. It was claimed by the
Wreck Commission and sold or dealt to local buyers. I
was one of the buyers. I bought cloth and threads.
Very good quality. Some pieces were very beautiful.
(Takes a piece from his pack) Look how the light shines
through this rare piece. Who will be the lucky household
to have this hang at their window? Which beautiful
woman will have this flow around her shoulders. But
in this country, they are set in their own ways. The same
as in my country, just in different ways. The same everywhere in the world. But here, it is white lace at the
windows and cotton for dresses. And no fancy shawls …
no not here. Although it would make the women look
even more beautiful against their pale white skin, their
red hair and green eyes. This whole shore *(Waves his arm)*
is all Irish. All Irish. Their speech is gentle, song-like.
They are a curious people. Curious to me and curious
themselves about me and the outside world. They have
been here for almost two centuries, sent out here, so they
tell me by the merchant Sweetman from Waterford to
farm and fish and cut wood. They are happy to be here,
their homeland was no better than my own, still is no
better. A civil war, no land to call their own, poverty, no
education. At least here, our children can have a chance
at something better. But the winters, oh, the winters.
What we all would not give for some time in the old
countries. Better not to think of that now, while the birds
sing and the road calls and my pack is full.

SOLO There are more and more of us coming here now.
And I heard talk at old Noah's store last week that the
peddlers are reaching out across the island. There are
branch stores now at regular intervals along the railway
lines. Us Lebanese are sent to places I have never heard
of, like Gambo, Glenwood, Grand Falls, Deer Lake,
Curling and St. George's, to manage stores. We are

setting up businesses for ourselves, but me ... I am not ready yet. I like this freedom. I am better with the language. Yes? But I need to understand the people more, their ways, their speech, their religion. I do not want to settle until I know them. And now, I am very close to a strange one. A very strange bird ... no, she is not a bird, she is ... What is she? This strange creature ... a troll? A beaver? *(Lights down)*

Lights up on Solo and a heap of rags on the floor. The heap twitches. Then there is more movement and a grunting sound. Suddenly the heap stands up and becomes a woman, an old crone. A walking stick pokes out from the heap of rags that cover her. The stick probes the floor, tapping like the cane of a blind person. She is coughing, spitting and scratching. She shuffles across to the old stove and keeps herself busy there. She looks out the window and sits down at the table. She drinks her tea and eats a piece of bread. Off in the distance the drawn-out sound of a foreign song gets louder.

KITTY Hmm ... that'd be himself.

There's a knock on the door.

KITTY Come in if you're blessed, and stay out if you're damned.

Solo enters and bows from the shoulder with a dip of his head.

SOLO Good morning, madam. Am I too early? Do I catch you unawares?

KITTY Do you catch my underwears? I hope not, Mr. Solo. I sincerely hope not, Mr. Solo honey.

SOLO Sorry?

KITTY I don't know where you got your English, Mr. Solo, but it certainly wasn't from us islanders. Sit down, Mr. Solo, and take a cup of tea with me.

SOLO Miss Kitty Bowe, thank you very kindly. And did you know, Miss Kitty Bowe, that I know some of your Irish? The language, I mean.

KITTY Then you know more than me, Mr. Solo, my dear. You must be talking to ole Tramore or to old Mrs. Tobin, or was it the old man Brennan? They all still have a smattering of the Irish while I ... well, I have a few prayers, and a few curses, I suppose.

SOLO So you can't say you have no Irish, Miss Kitty Bowe. Mmmm ... the tea is good and strong and hot.

KITTY The only fit way to drink it, sir.

SOLO The only fit way to drink it, madam.

KITTY No wonder you are so good at the English, Mr. Solo sir. All you does is repeat.

SOLO It is to get use to your flow of words, madam. If I repeat it, soon it will stick up here. *(Taps his temple)*

KITTY You should be a school teacher, Mr. Solo sir. You're that smart.

SOLO Oh, I would not say that. In my country I am not thought smart. I am only a peasant.

KITTY A pheasant?

SOLO Yes, a peasant.

KITTY Like what roams over the barrens and is good to eat?

SOLO *(Shocked)* I do roam, madam, but I hope I am not so tasty please.

KITTY Well, have no fear, Mr. Solo honey. You are safe with me. I dare say you are tough as old shoe leather any the how. So tell me now, what is all the newses?

SOLO Ah, the newses? Well, there's war, famine, pestilence, one person killing another because their religion is different ...

KITTY All up and down the Shore here?

SOLO In the world, Miss Kitty. In the great wide world.

KITTY Oh, the world be dammed, Mr. Solo honey. What do the world got to do with me? I means the Shore, sir. What is all the gossip, all the dirt and damage all up and down the Shore, sir, is what I wants to know.

SOLO *(Eyes her warily)* But you know, Miss Kitty Bowe, it would not look good upon me to talk of my customers. If I talk of them to you ... then perhaps I talk of you to them ... ah?

KITTY Oh, you're a smart one all right, Mr. Solo sir. But sure, can't you take a pity on a poor ole spinster woman who is all alone on this old bit of dirt road? Can't you find it in your heart to let fall a drop of ole something or other about someone or other between here and there? A morsel?

SOLO A morsel? What is this, a morsel?

KITTY A crumb, a speck of gossip. Twould be like sugar in me tea, sir, and give me something to ruminate on in the long evenings.

SOLO A morsel to ruminate on ... like sugar in your tea.

KITTY Who's doing what to who, Mr. Solo? Surely to God, in your country the peoples gossip?

SOLO Gossip? Oh, yes, I have never met a peoples who does not gossip.

KITTY *(Slams her hand on the table and Solo jumps. She pours him more tea.)* There, you said it. So, Mr. Solo, if you wants to fit in along this Shore then, sir, dig us up a bit of dirt.

SOLO *(Moves closer to her in a conspiring manner)* A bit of dirt? Well, I saw this morning, Miss Kitty, that the old man McGrath was turning his soil and planting his seed potatoes. He was digging up his dirt. *(Smiles)*

KITTY Digging up his dirt? Digging up his dirt? Ah Christ, Mr. Solo, you got me repeating you now. That's not gossip, sir. That's not dirt. That is … that is … common, ordinary, back-breaking work. The same as any soul would do this time of year. Ah, Mr. Solo honey, you're a bad man for the newses. What have you in your pack then, sir? Something more entertaining than your talk, I do hope. With all due respect, sir.

Solo bows his head and goes to the door to bring his pack to the table side. He takes his time unlacing the many straps that hold the pack together.

KITTY That's a mighty pack you have there, sir. I would think it could hold all the wonders of the world. Have you been lucky with any shipwrecks lately? *(Blesses herself)*

SOLO My luck is the world's misfortune, madam.

KITTY A strange way to make a living, sir. But an honest way, in its own way.

SOLO If the goods were not salvaged from the water, Miss Kitty, then what good would they be to the sea? The fishes do not sew with thread. The great whales do not wear the finery I carry. The seabirds have no use for pots and pans.

KITTY *(Laughs)* Oh, Mr. Solo, you do talk fanciful. Like the old bards back in Ireland. You must have kissed the Blarney Stone.

SOLO The Blarney Stone?

KITTY Yes, a stone near a great castle in the village of Blarney in County Cork. It is said that those who kiss it will have the gift of poetic speech, never be at a loss for words.

SOLO Could I kiss it in English? To get better English? *(He takes out a fine piece of red silk and holds it up to the window.)* Beauty, madam, beauty from out of a peddler's pack.

KITTY Oh, my, Mr. Solo. It do catch the light something grand, don't it? Oh my ... but what use would I have for something beautiful? Look around you, sir. In this hovel?

SOLO We have a saying in my country, Miss Kitty, that one thing of beauty makes the world beautiful.

KITTY Yes, well, that may work in your country, sir, but it would take more than one item here. And what would I do with that ... if I could afford it?

Solo goes to the front of stage and holds it under the light so that it shimmers. Kitty sighs at the beauty of it.

KITTY Oh, it is a thing of beauty, sir. A rare thing of beauty indeed. *(She stares and stares at it, as if in a trance. Then she pulls herself together and shakes herself out of it.)* What a case of the studies you had me in there! But ... have you any threads, sir ... threads so I can sew up my old rags for another season's use?

SOLO *(Sighs, folds the beautiful material and goes over to his pack. His back is turned to the audience and to Kitty.)* When you were young, Miss Kitty Bowe, if you will pardon my asking ... you were beautiful and you must have had a beau?

KITTY *(Falls back into the trance that the beauty of the material put her in earlier)* A beau? Hmmm … well, yes, I … I did, sir, as a matter of fact. And aren't you the spook? I do believe I was thinking on him in a dream last night.

SOLO *(Sits down. He has a small vial of something. He uncorks it and offers it to Kitty.)* Here. Smell. This is the scent of mandarins from my country. It is said to evoke memory and maybe it is a bit like your Blarney Stone, madam.

KITTY *(She leans in to smell the scent. Her eyes close and she smiles shyly.)* You are a trickster, sir. All them things of beauty. It can unnerve a lonely woman like myself. So then, I'll tell you a tale, Mr. Solo sir, but if I do, then you must tell me one too. A tale of you.

SOLO A tale of me? A tale for a tale. That is better than an eye for an eye.

KITTY No, none of that. This is a tale of love and not war, Mr. Solo honey. But before I tell, you must join me in a drop of poteen. For there was never an Irish tongue loosened without it, stone or no stone. And I do not like to drink alone. *(Goes to the cupboard and takes down two glasses and a jug. She fills two tumblers and they toast.)* May you be half an hour into the gates of heaven before the devil knows you're dead!

Solo says a toast in Arabic.

KITTY I was eighteen years of age, and yes, Mr. Solo, I do believe that I may have had a bit of the beauty about me. Or so they said in my village anyway. But no matter about that, one way or the other, for it did me no good, I tell you. My family was born into troubled times in the old country. We were fed up with the ways of the British. How they took everything from us, our land, our food, our language. My father was a Fenian, a proud Fenian in the county of Wexford. His father had fought and died in the uprising, one of the proud and famous "Pikemen of '98." My father had that legacy and he defended it. He escaped to this rugged shore, my father did, and hid out a few coves up, because he was a marked man after that association, after what his father did, see? And well, if truth be known, he did his own deeds for the honour of Ireland. Old Sweetman hid him aboard his boat and set him up out here. He met my mother, a Ryan from one of the islands in the bay, and he brought her out here. I was born here, but when I was seventeen I went back to the island where my mother was born, to visit with her. While there, I met a boy, he was from one of the other islands in the bay. What they call a Protestant island, or a Protestant part of that island, because really, all the islands were a mix of both and … they mixed well. But my father, well he never mixed well with the English, with the Protestants. He held onto the old hurts from the old ways. But the people out in the bay were different, they mixed, they accepted one another. They had to, see. They had to leave the old ways home. It was an unspoken rule somehow, how the people silently wanted things to work, you know?

SOLO Yes, a dream.

KITTY More than a dream. It had entered some vital part of them, this need. It was silent, but it was there. Anyhow, we met, my young man and me. My mother saw it and my grandmother saw it. Granny never thought nothing, but Mammy knew Da. Mammy watched the whole fortnight. While we walked, he and me. We walked the hills of the island. We got to know one another.

SOLO And he was a good young man, your beau?

KITTY Good? What do the young know about good?

But yes, of course he was good. I was no fool, I suffered no fools. Good, yes, and handsome too. With a square jaw running just so. And dark eyes the depth of wells. I tell you he had the manner of a duke or an earl, but the spirit of a rambling boy of pleasure.

SOLO A fine balance of a combination, I'd say.

KITTY A fine balance indeed, Mr. Solo. And we walked, investigating the small flowers of the bog. Isn't it a wonder how love draws out the common curiosities of the world and magnifies them? How, if you and I say, were walking on the barrens here, we'd not have the same look at the curiosities as we'd have with a lover, say?

SOLO *(A look of sadness on his face)* Yes, indeed, I'd say that. There is a … how do you say … a transforming quality to love, Miss Bowe.

KITTY A transforming quality? You are a scholar, Mr. Solo sir. Indeed a scholar.

SOLO No, a pheasant, remember, madam? Love does not need schooling. It only needs to be … ah?

KITTY To be? Well, yes that is all very well and good, but tell that to my father. If he was still among the living, that is.

SOLO And so your love story is a tragedy then? What happened?

KITTY Nothing. And that is the thing. Nothing enough. He was a fisher and worked at culling for the merchant. Skippered his own boat at thirteen years of age. Went back and forth over the seas to Portugal and Spain before I met him as a lad of eighteen. But I was an innocent. I came back to my father's house and I spoke openly of my heart around the cove. I called him by name, by last name, a Protestant one it was. And one evening after supper my father slammed his hand down on the table, looked me in the eye, and said, "We'll have no more of that." I did not have to ask him what "that" was. I dared not anyway because my father spoke so rarely to me that when he did, I knew every word for what it was. But still I snuck away … whenever the butter wagon was going to Placentia, or there was a herding of the cattle. I found an excuse to go and try and see my brown-eyed boy. And sometimes … sometimes we'd only see each other in passing. We'd only have a glance at one another. It was enough, for a while. Once we met for an entire evening tide. *(Looks shyly at Solo; he looks at her with a raised eyebrow.)* I got with child. *(Raises the other eyebrow)* What have you in them oranges, them mandarins? In that scent?

SOLO I only uncork the vial, madam. The magic is in the essence.

KITTY *(Defeated)* There you have it then, sir. My tragedy, my tale.

SOLO But the child? The love … baby?

KITTY Can we leave that for another time? Another tale? My heart is weary. I must lay down, Mr. Solo sir. Get back in under me ole bed of rags. I grow weary, sir. My heart, my heart.

Solo helps her to bed.

SOLO I am afeared, my good woman, that I have done you harm.

KITTY Never you mind. And didn't you say anyway, that it is the vials, the very essences, that do the work, sir? You are only a kind of host, a bearer.

SOLO But if I had not come … then your heart, your memories, would be your own.

KITTY And what good are they to me anyway? They are only a haunt that way. Now they are out there into the air, outside of my heart where they have wearied me for too long. You take them memories, Mr. Solo, and you pack them into your pack and dump them into the ocean, into the sea for me. I've carried them long enough. And now for my nap. And the threads, could you leave them on the table there? *(Reaches into her pile of skirts and drops coins into his hand)* And that lovely silk material ... I hope you find a young girl, one like I was once, who'd see you, sir, for the lovely man you are.

SOLO But a poor gossip?

KITTY Ah yes, but sure, you're a man, honey man. No man is a good gossip. Too bad, a good bit of gossip is a medicine, a cure. Especially if it is a good dirty bit. The dirty bit cleanses the soul, my dear man. And ah, don't you forget you owes me a tale, a story of your own.

SOLO Next time I'm here, Miss Bowe. I'll tell you of my country. A story with some sunshine in it. You sleep now. I'll find my own way out. *(He picks up his pack, takes the silk material out and streams it over the window. He looks back at the pile of rags, bows with his shoulders and a tilt of his head. He hoists up his pack, closes the door and exits. Lights fade.)*

Lights up. Solo is walking with pack on his back, whistling a song. He stops, takes off his pack, sits on it, takes out his handkerchief and wipes his forehead. He looks off into the distance as one looks out to sea.

SOLO What is it about people that makes some of them seem as if you knew them all your life? Miss Kitty Bowe is an old woman. I walk into her kitchen and it feels like I have been walking in there all my life. It could be my grandmother's kitchen. Not just the kitchen, the woman herself is familiar. We talk of nothing and everything. I think she trusts me. She tells me of her life, her troubles. She is a lonely old woman, but she knows who she is and is content with her lot. Maybe … maybe she is miserable with her lot. Her life has not been easy. She never married. Her heart was broken. Her child … I wonder where her child is. Well, I know all about leaving a child. Someday, I will tell her about my life in the old country. I'm glad that I left her that silk. Although I could get a pretty price for it. Still, I brought a light to her eyes just then. I would like that light to come back. Yes, tomorrow she will smile when she sees that piece of silk!

Solo looks up and sees a young woman coming up the path. She is swinging a wooden milk pail and is in her bare feet. She is singing an old ballad. She stops and looks at him and smiles. He stands and bows to her.

NANCY Good day to you, sir. Isn't it a fine day we're having?

SOLO Yes, madam! Yes. Yes. Yes.

She smiles at him in puzzlement, curtsies and moves on. Solo watches her go while crumpling the hat in his hands.

SOLO What an idiot! What a huge idiot I was! To not say anything sensible, like, what is your name. What an idiot! What a beauty! What an idiot! What a beauty! Such an idiot I am!

Solo wanders off the stage. Lights fade.

Lights up on Kitty's kitchen. Nancy and Solo sit at the table. Kitty is moving around the room.

KITTY Well, Mr. Solo honey, I never thought I'd see you so soon again.

SOLO It is about the material that I showed you yesterday. I wanted to make it a gift for you. That is why I left it here.

KITTY A gift ... for me? For here? This room? I don't think so, Mr. Solo sir. With all due respect. But thanks anyway.

SOLO But you liked it, Miss Bowe. It made you smile. I saw.

KITTY Made me smile? Did you hear him, Nancy? Did you ever hear the like? But, Mr. Solo, it was only bewilderment was the look on my face. At seeing such a fine piece of a thing, is all. And he had me transfixed yesterday, Nancy, he did. Telling him all kinds of old tales, I was.

Nancy appears nervous and shy. Kitty looks from Nancy to Solo and back again.

KITTY Oh, so that's the way it is. My kitchen is a courtin' kitchen now, is it?

Both Nancy and Solo remain stiff and say nothing.

KITTY Oh, so the young have no speech to them now, is it? Oh, they can be all gab when they knows it all, but when courting season opens up, well aren't they all hush, hush. So come, Mr. Solo, then, what is all the newses?

SOLO *(In a high-pitched voice from nervousness)* Newses, Miss Kitty? None, madam, no newesses at all esses.

KITTY And, Nancy? What's all the newses with youses?

NANCY Nothing much, Miss Kitty. Excepting Father lost another calf this spring and that has set him back and, and, and, fish is low and flour is high. So Mammy says.

KITTY And so youse is not married. And himself is not married, is that right, Mr. Solo man?

SOLO What? Married? To you, Miss Kitty? Honey?

KITTY *(Roars with laughter)* Oh, he do catch on fast, don't he, Nancy? Catch on to the joke. But it's no joke, Mr. Solo. Two single young people sittin' up stiff as yarrow in my kitchen is a sign of something amiss.

NANCY Miss Kitty, don't be talking like that. I don't know that man at all, sure. I mean, I knows nothing about you at all, sir.

KITTY What's there to know? There's something running between ye two, and more marries for less than that. If ye don't know each other, then why don't the two of ye be out walking and getting to know each other. And stop using my kitchen to be eyeing each other out of the corner of your eyes. So go on, get. I've cleaning to do and ye've hay to make while the sun shines. You hang on to that bit of material now, Mr. Solo honey. It's not me'll be needing that.

Kitty takes the silk down from the window, folds it, lays it on the table and bustles the two out the door. She sits down at the table.

KITTY I wonder what I'm starting there. Sure, I don't know him at all. He could be the devil himself. But no, some people you just know like you've knowed them all your life. He's like that. And I think he really did mean to give that beautiful silk material to me. Imagine that! That takes some kind of heart, that do. To think kindly on an old woman like myself. And he's a hard worker ... not a drinker. He's foreign, but sure, aren't we all to one another? Well, we'll see what her mother'll say to all this. I expect by the time she knows it'll all be done anyway. And sure, where's the harm in that? As long as he don't be taking her off to no foreign parts, but stays here on the Shore then, sure, there's no harm. There was worse matches made among them that knows one another.

Well, it's out of my hands now anyway. It's not my doing either. They'll make their own way without me or anyone. Sure, isn't love a force of nature? I say go with it while it lasts. *(Lights fade)*

Lights up on Solo and Nancy walking.

SOLO Are we making hay, Miss Nancy?

NANCY *(Laughs)* Don't think she don't have her spyglass up to her window, Mr. Solo.

SOLO Joe ... call me Joe. I'll call you Nancy?

NANCY Yes, Nancy. But is that your name ... I mean where you're from?

SOLO No, there I am Sulieman Yousif Saleh.

NANCY Sulieman Yousif Saleh. And I am Nancy Mary Agnes Foley.

SOLO And would you think about being Nancy Mary Agnes Foley Solo?

NANCY I do think I would think on that, Mr. Solo. But I'd like a fair bit of talking amongst us first, along with a bit of thinking on my own. If it's a rush you're in, Mr. Solo, perhaps you should keep walking.

SOLO I beg your pardon, Miss Nancy. I was only afraid you'd run off. But that is my intention ... to marry you. If you want more walking and talking, then I'll walk to the ends of the roads. Only my talking is not so good.

NANCY It is good. But there are some things ... if you'll excuse me, but what religion are you, Mr. Solo?

SOLO Religion ... I was born into the Druze faith. Many think that I am a Jew, but I am not a Jew. More call me a Turk. In Placentia, they call me Joe the Turk.

But I am not a Turk. But maybe I am not a Druze anymore either. I am here. Now this is my home. It is where I want to stay. There is no war here. You are here. It is very simple. Simple, like how when I first saw you and I thought ... she is the one I want to live with. The girl singing and swinging her pail of milk in the afternoon sun. I am not a complicated man, Miss Nancy.

NANCY Perhaps not complicated, but certainly interesting, Mr. Solo. And do you like this shore, sir?

SOLO Like it? Yes, I like it. In my country there are many people everywhere. We are crowded in among each other and fighting for space, and the fight is an old fight and it will go on. It is the wildness and the loneliness that I like here. A man can set himself apart. A man can try something new. Someday I want to put my pack down and open a store and sell what I sell from my pack from my own shop. I want to be a good businessman.

NANCY Like you are a good peddler. The people on this shore like you. I have heard your name long before I met you. But my father and mother must meet you and I'm thinking that if you keep walking out with me that you must consider changing your religion, sir.

SOLO I would go to your church, Nancy ... if your church would have me.

NANCY Let's go slow, Mr. Solo ... Joe. There is much to consider. *(Lights fade)*

Lights up on two men standing on the stage looking off into the distance.

MR. FOLEY No, it is not a good year for the fish, Mr. Solo. And even if it was, there is no price for it. I'd say you're in the better trade yourself.

SOLO But my trade depends upon your trade, sir. If you do not make money, then your wives cannot buy my threads, buttons and fabrics.

MR. FOLEY Ah ... so it is. Well now, I never knew I had another man depending on my luck, or the merchants' whims. And where do you be getting your goods, sir, if you don't mind my asking?

SOLO A fair question. Well, there are the merchants on Water Street that supply me. I buy from them and sell to you. Or else a shipwreck of goods, where I still have to buy, but the price is much less for me to buy that way.

MR. FOLEY Shipwrecks, is it? And had you anything to do with the *Florizel* that went down off Cappahayden last year? What I mean to say is, did you get any goods off her? Not that you would have had anything to do with the sinking like.

SOLO No, I did not. I did not get any goods from the ship ... nor did I have anything to do with her going down. *(Smiles and nods)* That was a great loss of life, and her cargo was only fish, I believe.

MR. FOLEY Fish products, yes. Twelve thousand barrels of it, worth over two hundred and fifty thousand dollars. Not a small loss, along with the tragedy of the hands lost. It was fifteen miles north of Cape Race and they said that the weather was fine enough starting off, but a storm brewed and before midnight it turned to a bad blizzard. It was in February, I do believe. I remember it was, because it was talked about by the men out that it was one of the worst storms they'd ever seen. She piled up on the rocks off Cappahayden, it was. The captain was William Martin, a fine skipper with a crew of six and seventy-six passengers. They say that the next morning all of Cappahayden woke to the shriek of the *Florizel*'s sirens. When the men went out there was no one on deck and bodies were already washing ashore. Later that evening, a few forms were found in the forecastle and more found mid-ship. Only about half a dozen found alive that day, and by the next day they totaled forty. How they managed to stay alive in the water, I don't know.

SOLO Shipwrecks must be plentiful on this shore too, sir?

MR. FOLEY We had our share off the Virgin Rocks here. And bodies come ashore and found treasure. Now, I'll tell you something: my great-grandparents were Nellie Bowe and Tom Foley. He had the nickname of Tramore because that's where he come from in Ireland, in the county of Waterford. Now, my great-grandmother's sister, that was before my time of course, well they say that she use to go down to the beach every day to gather driftwood for her fire. And this one morning when she left the house it was freezing hard. She took her axe and headed down to the beach, and she wasn't long out when she come upon some sticks jutting out of a pile of ice on the sand. She began to chop at the ice to get to the sticks when she saw she was chopping at clothing. She kept cutting into the ice and then she stopped when she saw she was hitting on the body of a man. She dropped her axe and went looking for help, and a couple of men come and found that it was the body of a foreign sailor. There was no identification on him so they built a wooden cross and buried him and put a cross over the site up there on the hill. So, I suppose there was more shipwrecks one time then there is around here these days. Any shipwrecks where you come from, Mr. Solo?

SOLO Shipwrecks? Oh no, sir. No shipwrecks, no water. We are a desert. We have only wars where I come from.

MR. FOLEY And is that why you left your homeland then?

SOLO I left because the Turks took over and we did not want that. I did not want to be ruled by Turks.

MR. FOLEY And so you come here to get away from someone, just like my grandfather come here to get away from the English. Well, let's hope we are not chased out of here then, Mr. Solo. And are there many of your people over here now?

SOLO A good many have been coming these past thirty years. Most went to North Sydney in Nova Scotia. There are some on Bell Island and more in St. John's. The Lebanese merchants in St. John's supply me when I need supplies. Mr. Kalleem Noah on Water Street is a great friend to the peddler. As well as Mr. Basha.

MR. FOLEY So, Mr. Solo, you are not a Jew or a tally man?

SOLO A "tally man"? Ah yes, you mean an Italian? No, I am Lebanese, not a Jew, not tally man. Although they are fine people for themselves.

MR. FOLEY And so all this time we all thought you were a Jew or a tally man or a Turk. Now the Jew, well he is Jewish, and the Italian, well, they got the Pope there in Rome, so they are all Catholics … and the Lebanese …

SOLO Druze is my religion. We are Muslims. We speak Arabic, Mr. Foley.

MR. FOLEY Oh, ah … well, that is a lot of different things, Mr. Solo. A lot of complications.

SOLO No complications, Mr. Foley. I can adapt. Speaking of Rome, you have an expression … when in Rome … I can adapt, Mr. Foley. I intend to make this shore my home and I would like to make your daughter my wife.

MR. FOLEY Well, she could do worse, Mr. Solo, despite you being foreign. With all due respect. My three daughters are good girls. A bit on the romantic side perhaps, with stars in their eyes. Their mother had them reading, you see. And all they do be talking about is far-off places. I suppose you've romanced one of them. I'll talk to her mother, Mr. Solo.

SOLO Thank you, Mr. Foley.

New interior scene. A year or more has passed. Solo and Nancy are married and they have children. Nancy is at the table making bread. Solo is in chair by the stove.

NANCY Perhaps if I'd have knowed that in your country you could have as many as four wives, I would have thought our marriage over.

SOLO So, you are sorry that you married me?

NANCY No, I am not sorry that I married you. You are a good man and a good father. But I am sorry that you got both my sisters with children too.

SOLO But your sisters are not sorry.

NANCY That is besides the point. This kind of thing is not done here. A married man takes only one woman to his bed ... their bed ... the marriage bed.

SOLO But I did not force your sisters. And you knew ... I know you knew.

NANCY *(With hesitation)* Yes, I knew, or I suspected. You are a charmer, Joe Solo. Aren't you? Like the snake charmers, you can hypnotize.

SOLO But Esther is married now to a good man who will take care of them both. And she knows she can come to us if she needs help. I would never turn away your family. Your family is my family. And Ellen has moved here to help out with all our babies and now has her own baby ...

NANCY By you! When will it stop, Joe?

SOLO You have no more sisters.

NANCY For God's sake, Joe! Do I have to run out of sisters for you to stop fornicating?

SOLO But I have never kept anything from you, or them. I have taken care of you, and would them if they needed me to.

NANCY Just tell me this ... did you do the same over there ... over in your own country before you came here? Did you have a wife? Did you get her sisters with children?

SOLO No.

NANCY No to which? Did you have a wife? Did you get her sisters pregnant?

SOLO No, I did not get her sisters pregnant.

NANCY What! You had a wife over there? You were married? You're a bigamist?

SOLO But I did not get her sisters with children. *(Pause)* She had no sisters.

NANCY *(Slaps down the dough on the table)* Oh Christ. I give up. Have you no conscience at all? Don't you realize that this means that we are not legally married? That our children are ... are bastards!

SOLO I may be a lot of bad things in your mind, and in your country, but do not call our children names. Nor your sisters' children names. In God's eyes they are gifts, and they are that to me also.

NANCY In God's eyes! In God's eyes! But the priest knows ... everyone knows. Tell me, Joe, have you been with others, outside of my family?

SOLO No, I have not, Nancy. And if this bothers you so much, I will stop.

NANCY Yes, well, that's very devoted of you, but I've run out of sisters.

SOLO *(Takes her in his arms)* I am yours.

NANCY And Esther's and Ellen's ...

SOLO But they do not want me, not like you want me.

NANCY You could charm the sun down from the sky, couldn't you Sulieman Yousif Saleh?

A man from the community is repairing his net at the front of the stage.

MAN You see, we all knew what was going on. The thing is, no one was getting hurt. I mean it's different *(Pause)* ... yes, it's different all right. But like, if I went over there, over to his country, wherever it's to he's from ... well, then I'd have to take a couple of wives there, right? That's the way I looks at it. Live and let live so. Now I'm not saying that the crowd around here like's it. I mean in Branch we're all Catholics. Always were and always will be. And we don't go in for that stuff, the couple of wives stuff, I mean. Most 'ed say one is plenty enough, more than enough. And the priest had to go talk with him. Tell him to haul in his reins, so to speak. I think he listened to the priest too, after that. But sure, you couldn't meet a nicer kind of man. No, sir, you could not! He goes to the mass and all now. Oh yes. And when he came here first he rented a house from Peter Willie. And then he had one built by William Roche, the grandest house in Branch, sure. And a barn to go along with it and kept horses as well as cows. Imagine! Not every man can say that now, can they? And he came here with only a pack on his back. And that's the real truth. Only a pack on his back. And now he with two stores here in the place. Two now, mind you! And him with only a sprinkling of a few words of English. I'd say his English is better than the magistrate's now. Two stores, one at the bottom here and the other as you're coming into Branch. Mostly food he sells but no … that's not true. The wife says he got it all in there now. I never goes in. I can't stand stores, buying stuff like. Hates it. She does all that. And he a power block of a man. Short and squat like a pack of bricks. And healthy! Oh my, he'd eat anything. I minds one time when we were having a talk about the fish … down by Nash's, we were, and he'd reach down and eat the grass like. Well, it wouldn't be the grass grass, but any old green stuff at all, and he knew the names for it all. Watercress he'd call the stuff, and mint he'd make into a tea he toldt me. And mushrooms. He never grew up with the fairies, see. Had no fear of them living under the mushroom caps and all. He'd gnaw on raw vegetables too, carrots and turnips and cabbage. Said it was better for you. He could be right. He'd drink the liquid, the liquor off the Sunday dinner too. Say that was the best part of it. Queer ways. And he keeps three white geese and they as pure white as the driven snow. I don't know what he wants with them, but he keeps them anyway. There was a shipwreck off here and Solo went and got the goods off her. He wasn't afraid of the water at all, although he never fished except for salmon and trout kind of thing. His wife was my grandmother's sister. Nancy Foley she was, Solo's wife. Good-looking woman. All them Foleys are good-looking women.

Suppose that had something to do with it ... I dunno. Takes all kinds, don't it? Wha? Sure, maybe half the people are jealous of him ... I dunno. What he did never kept people from going to his shop because he had the best merchandise, see. Cute enough, isn't he? Afraid of nothing. One time we were all out hunting together, hunting ducks, and it was the winter, see, and the water was so cold that the dogs wouldn't go in the water after the ducks that we shot, it was that cold. And what did Solo say to us but to put a line on him and he'd go after the ducks. Into the freezing water where the dogs wouldn't go! "Put a line on me and I'll go," he said. We wouldn't. He mighta been tough, but no one would last in that water, line or no line. Oh my, he was some mad at us. He kept shaking his head and jabbin' his fists in the air and lookin' out at the ducks bobbing on the water. Oh he was disgusted with us then, he was. But then bad things started to happen ... at the beginning it wasn't so bad, but then it turnt bad enough, that's for sure.

In the kitchen.

NANCY *(Standing at the door, yelling outside)* Make sure ye stay clear of that mash. And, Austin, you look after the younger ones. Simon, don't you dare go handy to them cliffs. Ye hear me? Do you? *(Turns and goes over to the table and talks to herself and the audience)* Oh they hear all right, but do they listen? I hope they'll mind each other and especially look after young Muriel, Ellen's girl. Well, Joe's girl ... and mine too, I suppose. She is a smart little one, that Muriel, and she watches her father do the accounts. Watches him like a hawk. She'll end up with a shop of her own one day, I'd say. Business is good now. We have a steady stream of customers, and they all know us and like us here. Sure, it was only up the road for me to go, but I often thinks on it, how hard it must have been for Joe, all this way from his home, or his "homeland," as he calls it. All the different food they eat there, things I'll only ever know be name. Grape leaves. Imagine! Lentils? Chickpeas. I like that name. Saffron. That's nice-sounding too, ain't it? Herbs and spices. I don't think I'd go for all that strange stuff, but I wouldn't mind some of them oranges he's been talking about all these years. And pears growing on trees, imagine? And olives, he says. And palm trees with palm oil. Oh my, and all that sun. We could use a bit of that. But I wonder what his first wife was like. Tamimi. She was killed by the Turks, and so now we are to have a visitor all the way from his homeland. His son ... Yousif Sulieman Saleh. Joe has heard from his brother over there and they say that Yousif is running wild through the Middle East. His brother says Joe has to do something with Yousif, and so we're having him shipped over here. I wonder how that will be.

Lights fade on Nancy as she exits. Up on Solo sitting by the stove eating nuts. He eats them fast, tossing them into his mouth. He looks at the audience.

SOLO I don't know what to do with him. This young man perplexes me, saddens me. We brought him here, Nancy and myself, and my brother guiding him through the paperwork. But he could not settle. Same as back in the homeland. He roams. His mind, his body. He did not want to learn English, kept speaking Arabic in the shop. Imagine! He refused to learn. He was hostile to my customers. Oh, I knew what he was saying to them. I am glad they did not. And he did not care if he took their money or gave the stuff away to them. But still, he did not like anyone here. He was causing my business harm, so I decided to open up a place for the young people to meet. I set up a pool hall so that he could mix with the local youth, but that did not work either. He refused to try to communicate. To learn English or to even engage them with our language. Always so angry. Nothing pleased or suited him. But then the last straw, as you say in this country, was when he attacked my wife. He went after her because of something she had cooked. It was a rage and certainly there was more to it than the mere food. But his anger was unfathomable. Deeper than the deepest well. We had to give in and declare our uselessness. We did not know how to help him. He did not want our help, only our presence to rail against. He tried to kill my wife. Perhaps he remembered his mother killed by the Turks. I certainly think of that. How I left them. What was I to do? Stay and join the army and fight the Turks? No, it meant death. I am sorry, Tamimi. I am sorry, Yousif. I am sorry, my wife, for my ways, my life pushed onto yours.

Nancy enters the house roaring.

NANCY Joe! Joe! Help me, Joe! The babies ... the babies! Joe! Joe! *(Black out)*

Nancy and Joe sit in the kitchen. There are three small coffins on the table between them. Man from the community walks past and says on his way out:

MAN Sorry for your troubles. *(Shakes hands with Solo and Nancy, walks out the door. There is a long silence as Nancy and Solo sit with their hands in their laps and their heads bowed.)*

SOLO I am sorry, Nancy.

NANCY *(Looks over at him quickly)* Sorry? You did not do anything. It was the mash that did it. The dirty water in the mash. They were poisoned by the water, Joe. We both know that. Everyone knows that. And I warned them. I toldt them. I did. But maybe I didn't tell them often enough. Maybe I didn't tell them that day, Joe.

SOLO Nancy, stop. You told them. It is not your fault. You told them and you looked out for them. You have been a good mother.

NANCY But not good enough or they'd be alive. I should have watched them, Joe. I should have given them water to drink before they went out to roam around.

SOLO So then we are both to blame, is that it? But I'm the worst. I'm the one who wanted you to have me, to have children with me. If I had never come here, you could have married a good local man and the children would still be alive.

NANCY What are you saying, Joe? They wouldn't be your children then. They wouldn't have been ours, our Austin, Simon, Joseph. You have been a good father. It is me who was negligent.

SOLO Negligent? You watched them like a hawk watches mice. The water was bad, Nancy. And children will drink and eat anything in sight. You did your best. But perhaps it is my curse, Nancy. Perhaps it is God's way of saying I have been a bad man, a bad father.

NANCY But you have not been a bad father, Joe. And you are not a bad man. Not ever.

SOLO But I have done hurtful things, bad things in the eyes of this country.

NANCY You came to this country with the ways of your country. You did things that I did not understand. But you stopped. You stopped for me. I would never see you as a bad man. We have built a life together and now our life has been torn apart.

SOLO Nancy, I have lived through poverty. I have lived through wars. I have lived through losing my country. But the loss of children makes all the rest seem like a dream that someone else had. That someone told me about.

NANCY (*Crying softly*) What are we to do, Joe? How am I to live now, when everywhere I turn, all I see are my babies. I cannot go to that door without expecting to see them running across that mash. That mash that has taken them from me. What can I do now except sit here forever and wait to die also?

SOLO No. We must not throw away the gifts we were given, Nancy. Would the babies want us to die too? No. We will have to start again. We have to depend on each other. *(Looks at her)* Tell me that you are ready to try again. *(She nods to him as the lights fade.)*

Lights up on Solo. There is a new tablecloth on the table, new curtains, etc., to show they are in a new place.

SOLO We had to leave. Not because it was a bad place. Branch was good to us. But how could we stay when everywhere we looked we saw our children running about. No one can live with ghosts. Ghosts inhabit the soul until one becomes a ghost themselves. A living dead. Nancy and I buried our children and we packed up our belongings. We sold the shop and the merchandise. I must remember to get the rocking chair to Mrs. Annie Nash, she asked for it. Corner Brook looks promising. There is a new pulp and paper mill going up, and people from all over the island are moving there. It is a good opportunity for a shop, or two, or three. And we are young, Nancy and myself. We will have more children. The world is a good place. The world is a big place. And I can move on, once again. I am a peddler after all. I can carry our world in my pack if I need to. I am a peddler once again, ready to buy and sell. Solo. Solo the peddler. *(Hoists his pack onto his back and slowly walks off the stage singing the Arabic song that he sang at the beginning.)*

ACKNOWLEDGEMENTS

Eleven years making a theatre troupe work depends on dedication, stubbornness and crazy love. No one showed more of that with Tramore than Arlene Morrissey, Tramore's administrator. Her contributions have been listed elsewhere, but here I would like to give a special thank you for her stick-to-it-iveness. Tramore's main actor, Mildred Dohey, has been with us all the way too. She has been brave and patient throughout, taking on each role (and switching gender) with grace and daring. All our board members throughout the years have given their time and talents so generously. They have been/are: Kevin Pittman, John Joy, Stan Dragland, Marnie Parsons, Marion Cheeks, Monique Tobin, Kate Evans, Calvin Manning, Michael Murray, John Cheeseman, Florence Careen Power, and Gemma Hickey.

The people of the Cape Shore and all of Placentia Bay have supported us by coming out to our shows every year. Also, my friends in the art world have made the trek out from town each summer. Janet Russell recorded our shows for the Alder Institute. Emma Butler supplied encouragement, and wine for the Saturday night dances (and danced herself). Eleanor Dawson believed in our work from the beginning and was instrumental in getting us early financial support, as was Anne Deveraux at the HRDC office in Placentia. The Newfoundland and Labrador Arts Council jumped in all the way, and Canada Council for the Arts, from up-along, understood our ideas, accents and all. Marie-Annick Desplanques made the original connection with the Bere Island group which linked Tramore with Ireland. Also there for us were: ACOA, Service Canada, Cultural Industries – Department of Tourism, Canadian Nature Federation, Important Bird Areas Program, Irish-Newfoundland & Labrador Business Partnership, Irish Newfoundland Association, INCO, Eastern Health, Eastern Health Wellness Coalition, Safety Net-Fishery Safety, Bere Island Community Committee, and New Horizon for Seniors.

Three important artistic influences whose voices rang in my head over the years are: the playwrights J. M. Synge and Martin McDonagh and filmmaker Mike Leigh. Their humour, bull's eye dialogue and love of language never cease to astound me.

Pamela Morgan has been friend and inspiration. Her link to the old traditions and love of the music and manners whenever she sings and works with Tramore keep me from despairing that all the old ways are dead.

My dear friend Mike McGrath, whose home in Patrick's Cove was everyone's home, taught me more than the oral history of the area. By being who he was, he extended his old world grace and sociability to all around him. He was spiritual father and teacher to me.

When my children would rather have been listening to heavy metal or staying in the city they came and sat on chairs in Mike's kitchen and learned of the old ways. I thank Patrick and Simone for their patience, and I watched with joy their interest grow for the area.

The people of the Cape Shore shared their stories and showed me the delight of the everyday lives of all they talked about. Their kindness and spirit are attributes to learn from. Thanks to Robert McGrath for his stories, especially about Patsy, Bride and Anthony.

Gemma Hickey read all the plays out loud to me, and she laughed and cried in all the right places, thus making me love them again. Her editing eye was a great help to me, as was the patience and eagle eye of Annamarie Beckel. Thanks to Rhonda Molloy for her hard work on designing the cover and the plays within. Rebecca, it is good to be with Breakwater. Thanks for wanting the plays.